THE
FIELD GUIDE
TO EXTRAORDINARY
COMMUNICATION
& CONNECTION

RACHAEL DOYLE

THE
FIELD GUIDE
TO EXTRAORDINARY
COMMUNICATION
& CONNECTION

Published and Distributed by

SOUND WISDOM
PO Box 310
Shippensburg, PA 17257-0310
717-530-2122

info@soundwisdom.com
www.soundwisdom.com

Cover/Jacket design by Eileen Rockwell

Interior design by Terry Clifton

ISBN 13 TP: 978-1-64095-078-8
ISBN 13 eBook: 978-1-64095-079-5

For Worldwide Distribution, Printed in the U.S.A.
2 3 4 5 6 / 22 21 20 19

Dedication

For Shawn, the love of my life.

Contents

CHAPTER 1

Welcome to the Field Guide to Communication and Connection

As Chief Operating Officer of New Light Learning and Development and home of Shawn Doyle Training, our team has come to realize that when many of our clients talk with us about an issue they have within their business, it's often not the issue they discuss—it's really about ineffective *communication*. That is the idea behind this book.

This book is not just about communicating, but rather how, where, and when to communicate in a way people will respond positively so you can be more effective, more productive, and really make a connection with people. This will be your "secret sauce" to being a better communicator, and more likely to being more successful, getting a promotion, and being much more effective at work and at home.

Communication doesn't necessarily always mean that you agree with someone's opinion—we can always agree to disagree. In today's world, communication should mean that even if you disagree, you should still be able to be respectful and kind in the hope that you can connect with other human beings. People can tell and feel your caring and authenticity.

Some people call effective communication: manners, etiquette, or being polite. Said perhaps another way, I am talking about respect or being kind in the way we communicate. Every form of communication—writing or verbally in person by phone, one-on-one, in group meetings, electronically on email, Skype, conference calls, text messages, and yes even Twitter, Facebook, and Instagram—involves critical at-work and life skills. As etiquette expert Judith Martin said, "Etiquette is all human social behavior. If you're a hermit on a mountain, you don't have to worry about etiquette; if somebody comes up the mountain, then you've got a problem. It matters because we want to live in reasonably harmonious communities."

The following are some interesting, compelling, and maybe some disturbing facts that tell us why effective communication skills are critically important:

- In a research study from Gonzaga University, it was found that people who say "Thank you" are perceived as having a warmer personality. The study claims that saying thank you starts new friendships, reminds people of their existing social bonds, and maintains older relationships.

- An overwhelming 95 percent of senior executives and managers surveyed by NFI Research feel that good manners matter when it comes to advancing a person's career, with two thirds saying good manners are extremely important. That's even more true of smaller businesses than large ones. Seven out of 10 executives in small businesses said that good manners were important in advancing a person's career compared to just over half (55 percent) of those in large organizations.

- Dr. Barbara Griffin, from the University of Western Sydney in Australia, has found that colleagues or mangers who are rude and undermining can have a demonstrable negative impact on employee engagement and productivity. She also found that one in five employees experience a significant incident of bad manners at work once a month.

- A survey by the Public Agenda Forum found 84 percent of survey participants believe a major cause of disrespect in American society today is too many parents failing to teach respect to children.

- Some 75 percent of Americans believe their smartphone usage doesn't impact their ability to pay attention in a group setting, according to the Pew Research Center, and about a third of Americans believe that using phones in social settings actually contributes to the conversation. (Note: This is so wrong!)

- A study in 2010 found that adolescents ages 8 to 18 spent more than 7.5 hours a day consuming media.

- In 2015, the Pew Research Center reported that 24 percent of teenagers are "almost constantly" online.

- Most adults spend 10 hours a day or more consuming electronic media, according to a Nielsen's Total Audience Report from 2017.

- David Grossman reported in "The Cost of Poor Communications" that a survey of 400 companies with 100,000 employees each cited an average loss per company of $62.4 million per year because of inadequate communication to and between employees. Debra Hamilton asserted, in her article "Top Ten Email Blunders that Cost Companies Money," that miscommunication cost even smaller companies of 100 employees an average of $420,000 per year.

- According to Watson Wyatt's newest communication survey for 2009/2010, companies that are effective communicators "have the courage to talk about what employees want to hear," "redefine the employment deal based on changing business conditions," and have "the discipline to plan effectively and measure their progress effectively." Does this really matter? Yes. The study shows that companies that communicate effectively had a 47 percent higher return to shareholders over a five-year period (mid-2004 to mid-2009).

- Survey respondents said the top priority for their communications department is ensuring employees feel informed and connected, yet nearly three quarters say they have problems keeping employees "on brand and on message" when communicating company news and information.

Employees agree—in fact, Gallup reported that 74 percent of employees are disconnected and feel that they're missing out on company information and news.

A 2014 Gallup survey asked 1,015 people how frequently they had used a variety of communication methods the previous day.

- Seventy-three percent of respondents said they had read or sent a text every day.
- Eighty-two percent had made a phone call on a cell phone.
- Seventy percent had sent or received an email, and 55 percent had used social media to communicate.
- Twenty-six percent of employees think email is a major productivity killer.

The following bullet points are interesting facts that I've discovered when researching this important subject:

- CareerBuilder provided lots of interesting stats about what employees think of email. When email became popular, it seemed like it was one of the best things to ever happen to businesses. Now that the honeymoon phase is over, it's clear that email isn't all it's cracked up to be. Inboxes get overwhelming. Lengthy chains get confusing and make it hard for people to locate the information they need. Group emails become distractions when everyone replies to the thread with unnecessary or irrelevant responses.
- Twenty-six percent of people feel pressured to respond to work communication outside

of work hours. This stat is one of many documented in the Cornerstone's The State of the Workplace Productivity Report. One of the greatest parts of having a wide variety of communication methods is that it makes everyone more accessible. But that can also be one of the biggest downsides. Nobody wants to spend their free time answering emails or returning work calls, but many people feel pressure to do just that.

- The Dynamic Signal report outlines the conflict between priorities and budgets. According to Gallup, disengaged employees cost the United States more than $500 billion each year in lost productivity. Organizations can improve productivity by up to 25 percent by connecting with employees, according to McKinsey. Additionally, Aon Hewitt reports that for every 1 percent increase in employee engagement, brands can expect to see an additional 0.6 percent growth in sales.

- A study performed by Pew Research Center asked a national sample of adults to select from among ten options the single skill that is most important for children to learn in order to succeed in the world, and 90 percent of respondents selected "communication" as their answer.

- "Effective internal communications can keep employees engaged in the business and help companies retain key talent, provide consistent value to customers, and deliver superior financial performance to shareholders," according to the Watson Wyatt Effective Communication 2009/2010 ROI Study Report.

- According to Talent Management, 86 percent of employees blame lack of good communication and collaboration for workplace failures. "The general consensus of the executives was that effective communication skills are more important now than ever before for business success," say researchers James Bennet and Robert Olney, "and these skills will continue to be a critical component of the information society."

- According to a January 2013 employer survey conducted by Hart Research Associates, 93 percent of employers consider good communication skills more important than a college graduate's major.

- According to Salary.com, the biggest waste of time, according to 47 percent of our respondents, is having to attend too many meetings. That's followed by dealing with office politics (43 percent); fixing other peoples' mistakes (37 percent); coping with annoying coworkers (36 percent); busy work

(22 percent); and returning an abundance of work emails (20 percent). Dealing with bosses came in last at a mere 14 percent.

- According to research from Harvard Business School and the London School of Economics, executives spend upwards of 18 hours per week—a third of their working week—in meetings. And with an estimated 25-50 percent of meeting time considered wasted, it's no wonder that meetings have become the number one irritation of many office workers. Software company Atlassian puts the cost of unnecessary meetings to United States businesses in terms of wasted salary hours at $37 billion.

But what about the cost to individuals?

- According to a 2012 survey by Salary.com "too many meetings" is the single biggest waste of time at work; up from #3 on a similar survey in 2008.

- A Microsoft Office Survey listed the top three time-wasters as: ineffective meetings, unclear objectives, and lack of team communication.

- The number of hours each week office workers spend in meetings; most feel that less than half of that time is productive. (Opinion Matters, for Epson and the Centre for Economics & Business Research; May 2012)

- 25% is the percentage of time spent in executive meetings, that estimates say, is devoted to irrelevant issues.

- 80% is the percent of meeting time, a Wall Street Journal article suggests, could be eliminated by following a detailed agenda.

- $37 billion is the amount of money the U.S. Bureau of Labor Statistics estimates that U.S. businesses lose in unnecessary meetings every year.

• • •

I was fortunate enough to be raised by a great family who taught me manners, kindness, empathy, and how to communicate effectively and to be polite. They did it by teaching me and modeling it themselves. I also was fortunate enough to have parents who were entrepreneurs. We would live in a small town in the Poconos of Pennsylvania part of the year and in Coral Gables, Florida, the rest of the time. Being in a small town and then in a big city taught me about communication and how people communicate differently. As I grew up and went to work for different companies, and later on owning my own business, I kept studying and learning. I worked at it because I knew it was important. It has always paid off personally and professionally.

The good news is you can learn to be a good communicator—and even a great one if you wish to be. It takes some study, training, practice, and most of all wanting to get better. Hope has arrived at least in one form—this book.

Here are a few things to reflect on about communication:

1. Communication needs to be about them. When people communicate, they need to be much more focused on the other person— and listen to them. Be focused less on your own wants and needs. If you use that precept when communicating with anyone on any communication channel, you will be much more effective.

2. The channel you pick matters. We live in a society where we are way too reliant personally and professionally on email or texts when the facts tell us that is the least effective form of communication. So many conflicts happen when people misinterpret the "tone" of a message. The reason this happens is they can't hear the words or see body language—they only read the words. We need to be more strategic about what we communicate and what channel of communication we use.

3. Know your goal. When creating any kind of communication, it's a good idea to know your goal. Before you communicate, think about what it is that you want. Do you want the other person to take action, think about something, change something? What is it?

4. Be nice. Okay, I know this is a really simple one, but the reality is if you can be nice, you will separate yourself from others who are not nice! It's a sad fact, but most people are surprised when you are nice. Let nice be your differentiator. It also makes life more enjoyable for them and you. People are much more likely to do something if you ask them and not tell them or demand it be done.

5. Don't let emotions rule. Many people when communicating let their emotions rule them. For example, they read an email, get angry, and "fire back" in a confrontational way. This often leads to an angry response and now we have—cue music dum dee dum dum...— conflict! If you are being too emotional, the best advice is to delay or defer until you can be rational. Then you will be a skilled communicator, not a "Wow, he really flipped out" communicator. People who are successful at communication have a high level of emotional intelligence.

6. Don't assume motive when communicating. This statement is easy to say but harder to do. Because you don't really know what someone's intent is, just ask questions. When you do, they will appreciate the fact that you want to know their intentions. They will know that you care about what they want or need.

In this book I divided the content into mini chapters. Each chapter is focused on a single subject so you can read the whole book, or just the chapter that you want to read, or several chapters at a time to help you with a specific communication issue.

Are you ready? Let's get started!

CHAPTER 2

In-Person
Communication Skills

*"Communication—the human connection—is
the key to personal and career success."*
—PAUL J. MEYER

Everyone has had the experience of meeting with someone and walking away with a positive impression or walking away with a sense that you didn't connect or something was not right. Why? There were some communication issues either on your part or the other person's part or both.

The other day I walked into a car dealership parts department to pick up something I had ordered for my car. Three people sat at their desks. When I walked in, no one looked up or greeted me. The person who finally waited on me never smiled and when I asked how his day was going, he gave me a pained smile and said, "It's going." I have a feeling I will not buy my next car there. I did not feel appreciated, valued, or let alone even welcome to do business there.

Here are some interesting facts about communication:

- Twenty-eight percent reported poor communication as the primary cause of failing to deliver a project within its original time frame, according to a survey by the Computing Technology Industry Association.

- Seventy-two percent of people say their impressions are impacted by how someone appears and their handshake.

- Remote meetings generate on average 10.43 ideas, while in-person meetings generate an average of 13.36.

- The good news is you can get better at in-person communication—it's a learned skill. Oh sure, some people are just better communicators than others. But I believe that effective communication in person consists of three areas, the Three C's:

1. Connection. Use verbal and nonverbal cues to connect, and try to understand where the other person is coming from.

2. Clarity: Say what you mean and mean what you say.

3. Context: Understand what is going on and communicate in the right context.

The following are twenty tips and tools:

Tip 1: Distraction action. When you are talking with someone one-on-one, try to eliminate distractions: 1) in the space visually; 2) in the space around you in terms of noise; 3) do not multitask; 4) guard against interruption (this is hard in the new world of open office spaces but do your best).

Tip 2: Body language. If you want to communicate effectively and connect, you need to be aware of *negative body language,* which include:

- Crossed arms
- Pointing at the other person
- Leaning back in your chair
- Bouncing a leg up and down
- Shaking head in disagreement
- Looking at nails
- Fiddling with items
- Looking at your watch or a clock repeatedly
- Standing too close

- Being too far away
- Slouching

Many studies have shown that up to 55 percent of communication is nonverbal, which is why it is very important to be aware of the nonverbal signals that you send. The next time you're in a meeting, ask a trusted colleague to observe your body language and give you feedback afterward. Do the same for the colleague if asked.

Tip 3:   The eyes have it. Research shows that eye contact is very critical for making connections with others. You can say a lot with your eyes. In fact, science shows that eye contact is a cornerstone of nonverbal communication between individuals. The mutual gaze is a "two-way street," a type of conversation "where each person signals as well as reads gaze information," write Michelle Jarick and Alan Kingstone in their 2015 research paper, "The Duality of Gaze." Eye contact is undoubtedly important, agrees David Keatley, Director of Researchers in Behaviour Sequence Analysis (ReBSA) at the University of Lincoln, UK. "Eye contact can tell us if someone is listening and attending to us. It can tell us we have their attention. It can then show their emotion—concern, enjoyment, happiness, love," he says. Work on making eye contact when you speak with someone. If you don't make eye contact, there are many implications about lack of trust or confidence. I know that some people aren't as comfortable with it, but it will serve you well to learn how. If you practice, you can do it! Maintaining eye contact is a critical skill for connecting with others.

Tip 4: Smile for the camera. When you're meeting with someone and smile, you can have a very positive impact on your interaction with the other person. But don't take my word for it, scientific research backs the idea of smiling to improve levels of communication. According to one study at the University of Scotland, when functional MRI machines measured emotional processing centers of the brain, people responded positively to the emotional stimulus of smiling, which activated the happiness circuitry of the brain. So when you meet someone and you naturally smile at the person, it creates a positive impression. They may not be consciously aware of it, but it does happen. We have always noticed that when professional speakers smile at an audience, the audience almost always smiles back even though they may not be aware of it.

Tip 5: Hello, friend. Even though it seems like a simple suggestion, one way to connect with other people is to just be friendly. When you are friendly, you receive a much better response from the person you're trying to communicate with. In a research report by Kelly Services, which was conducted with over 134,000 people, the trait that people identified as the most important were verbal communication skills. Even if you're not aware of it, we are subconsciously attracted to people who are friendly and likable. We are also subconsciously repelled by people who are unpleasant and rude. The words "please" and "thank you" go a long way in effective communication, especially if they are accompanied by a pleasant tone of voice and a smile (your mom was right). Mary Lambert said, "Treat others as you wish to be treated. Don't just be nice, but be kind to other people. That can be so rewarding."

Tip 6: We now pause for a commercial message. Pausing is a good idea when communicating with another person, to think and pause briefly before you speak. This actually has two advantages: 1) pausing allows you to think about what the other person said before responding; and 2) it also makes you more credible to the other person as being thoughtful about what was said.

Tip 7: Seek. In the book *The Seven Habits of Highly Effective People*, Dr. Stephen Covey wrote about the habit of seeking first to understand then to be understood. If you're having a conversation with someone and you first seek to understand the person *before* trying to make yourself understood, it will definitely make a positive impression. If you can make the conversation about the other person and less about you, the person will feel acknowledged, respected, and valued, and you will make more of a connection personally and professionally.

Tip 8: In the mirror. Another interesting aspect of communication research shows that people that are more likely to connect with people who are like them. That is the idea behind "mirror communication." If someone you are communicating with is more energetic, be more energetic; if someone is more reserved, you're a little more reserved. If the person speaks softly, you speak more softly. When you mirror the communication style, this makes the other person feel more comfortable and feel like making a connection with you. If you ever met someone you connected with and felt like they were your best friend, it is probably because the person was a lot like you! My best friend, Julie, and I have many of the same personality qualities and beliefs. A study at the University of the Netherlands found that mimicry increases goodwill and social orientation. Now this doesn't mean you change your personality completely, you are just trying to relate to people in their way.

Tip 9: Summary report. Another effective communication and connection tool is to summarize what you thought the other person said in your own words. This sounds something like, "Well, John, what I thought I heard you say is…. Is that correct?" This also helps to clarify what you heard was accurate or not; it shows you're interested in making sure that you heard correctly.

Tip 10: Shake it. In the world of business, the ability to shake hands properly and introduce yourself well is an important skill. Whenever you start a meeting, the first thing you should do after greeting the person in a positive manner is shake his or her hand. Most research on culture indicates that the custom of shaking hands began in medieval times, when people simply offered a hand to another to affirm friendship and that they were not armed and meant no harm. Shaking hands is a great way to make a connection, touching the other person in an appropriate way. Both men and women should shake hands with a slightly firm grip, making sure your hand meets web to web, making eye contact, and then releasing.

No limp-noodle handshakes and no crushing handshakes. If someone extends his or her left hand and not the right, shake the one offered. They may have an injury to their right hand. It is my opinion that fist bumps and high-fives are in the majority of the cases unprofessional and will make a negative impression, not a positive one. Research reported in the *Journal of Cognitive Neuroscience* shows that opening interactions with a handshake leads to positive social evaluations. Translation: If you shake hands, people will like you more.

Tip 11: Contract. One way of making sure you have an effective meeting with people is to contract with them. What this means is, at the beginning of the conversation you state your objective and ask them if they agree with the same objective that you mentioned. For example, you may say, "Walter, I think we can both agree that the reason for a meeting today is to try to work out solutions for the Smith account issue." If Walter agrees, then he is on board. It may also be good idea to contract with the other person about interruptions. One way of doing this is offer yourself as the first person willing to make the offer. You can say, "Since this is an important meeting, I'm not going to be interrupted, I am not going to answer my phone and I'm not going to look at my email. Can we agree that is a good idea for both of us?"

Tip 12: Internal noise. You read earlier in this chapter about avoiding distractions during your meeting with someone. One distraction certainly can be external noise, which sometimes cannot be avoided—but internal noise can be. Internal noise can either be a result of thinking about other things while the person is talking; or you could be so upset with what the other person is saying that you may shut down and listen more to *your emotions.* This can be a huge challenge for staying focused, but one that can be achieved if you work at it.

Tip 13: Assumptions. Another barrier to effective communication is to make assumptions about how the other person perceives the situation. The only way to really know how the other person perceives the situation is to ask lots of open-ended questions. Try not to automatically make assumptions. Wait until after your questions are answered before drawing any conclusions.

Tip 14: On a clear day. One interesting element in the business world is the use of jargon. It is amazing how some companies use tons of acronyms and abbreviations and words that new people in the organization do not understand. I find it hilarious that in some companies new employees are given a glossary of terms so they can understand what people are saying in meetings. As reported in a recent story, Elon Musk, founder of Tesla and Space X, sent out an email to every company employee that the use of acronyms needed to stop immediately or he would have to take drastic action. He wrote, "for example there should not be an HTS (horizontal test stand) or a VTS (vertical test stand) as they contained unnecessary words and were confusing." I have met company employees who have forgotten what the acronyms in the company stand for, but are too embarrassed to ask.

Tip 15: Thank you. It is amazing how powerful the phrase "Thank you" can be. You should use forms of appreciative language when communicating with other people. For example, you can say, "Joe, I really appreciate that you brought up that idea." Even if you disagree with the idea, you could show appreciation for someone coming up with an idea. When people get positive feedback, they want to communicate more. This is known as "affirmative communication."

Tip 16: These eyes. When you are communicating with another person observe the reactions of the other person. Sometimes people lack emotional intelligence, meaning they are not aware of how their actions impact the people around them. By simply observing, you can gain a lot of valuable information and can even give people feedback. For example, if you notice negative body language when you're meeting with someone one-on-one, you can say, "I could be wrong, but you seem to be a little frustrated. What other questions can I answer for you?" This will show that you are a masterful communicator who is observing the other person's responses.

Tip 17: Introductions, please. When meeting people, if possible, stand up. Always smile, introduce yourself using your first and last name, ask their name, and shake their hand. Use their name as soon as you hear it. Say, "It's nice to meet you, Julie." This will help you remember it later. Your handshake should be firm and confident and accompanied by eye contact. This is not the time to be shy. If you are travelling abroad and having meetings in another country, research the proper greeting protocol for that country and culture.

A few thoughts about attire; as mentioned earlier in this chapter, people do judge you based on how you look, so attire is an important part of effective communication and connection. The reality is that people believe what they see.

Tip 18: Know the code. Every company has written or implied dress codes. Know what it is and dress on the upper end of it. You should never underestimate how important appearance is. The best rule is to avoid being an example of how *not* to dress at work; be conservative. I have seen people at work who looked like they just rolled out of bed and came to work, and I've seen people who were dressed for the beach. As Miuccia Prada said, "What you wear is how you present yourself to the world, especially today, when human contacts are so quick. Fashion is instant language."

Tip 19: Attention please. You don't want to bring the *wrong* kind of attention to yourself because of attire. Clothes that are too tight, too short, too high, or too low cut should never be worn in the workplace. Be cautious of wearing too much cologne or perfume. Jewelry is fine in moderation. These tips apply to men and women.

Tip 20: The judge. Like it or not, people in leadership roles in your company will make judgments about you based on your appearance. They assume that how you dress is a sign of how you behave and of your professional credibility.

I believe you should dress like the position you aspire to get promoted to in the company. As Edith Head said, "You can have anything you want in life if you dress for it."

> *"Be kind. It's worthwhile to make an effort to learn about other people and figure out what you might have in common with them. If you allow yourself to be somewhat curious—and if you get into the habit of doing that—it's the first step to being open minded and realizing that your points of view aren't totally opposite."*
>
> —VIGGO MORTENSEN

Email Communication Clarity and Effectiveness

"The from line is what recipients use to determine whether to delete an email. The subject line is what motivates people to actually open the email."
–LOREN MCDONALD

Email seems to be the one tool which people have a love-hate relationship. We need it, we want it, and yet it can be a bit overwhelming at times.

Let's take a look at a few interesting statistics:

- According to research, by the end of 2019 it is estimated that there will be 2.9 billion email users worldwide. Research also shows that about 269 billion emails were sent and received every day in 2017.

- According to the most current research, the average office worker receives 121 emails per day.

- In the Holmes Report, David Grossman reports in his article, "The Cost of Poor Communication" that in a survey of 400 companies in the US and UK with more than 100,000 employees, there was an average loss per company of $62.4 million a year because of inadequate communication to and between employees.

So, I think it is obvious that email is an essential tool for communication both professionally and personally. But the question is, how can we communicate more effectively via email?

Here are some tips to improve and increase your email efficiency.

Tip 1: To be an email or not to be an email—that is the question. As the Chief Operating Officer of a training and development company, one thing that we say in our training programs is that "we need to be more thoughtful about email." What do we I mean by that? As odd as it may sound, there are times when an email may *not be* the best choice for effective communication. You may want to ask yourself if the message you're getting ready to send would be better served by a phone call, meeting with the person one-on-one, meeting with people in a group call, smoke signals, or Morse code. Well, you get the idea. What we find is, generally speaking, *email becomes the default form* of communication when it may not always be the best choice. After all, email is just written communication and we're missing important clues when we read an email such as tone, body language and facial expression. So, ask yourself if an email is even warranted. As Simon Sinek said, "A five-minute call replaces the time it takes to read and reply to the original email and read and reply to their reply...or replies. And I no longer spend 20+ minutes crafting the perfect email—no need to." Remember at all times that you are writing a *business* email and it should be concise and professional.

Tip 2: Be specific. When composing an email, be sure *before* you compose the email what your objective is. For example, the goal of emails is usually to ask or tell someone to: 1) do something; 2) change something; 3) come up with ideas; 4) deliver information; 5) answer questions. These are just a few examples of what the objective of an email could be. I often find that emails are confusing because the sender was not clear about the objective. After reading the email I was still unsure what they were trying to achieve. First, make sure you are clear about your goal even before you touch the keyboard. Second, *never put the sender's name in the "send to"* *box until you have finished composing the email.* That way you can never accidentally send an email before you are ready to send it.

Tip 3: What's your line? One of the most important aspects of any email is the subject line. Here are a couple of suggestions to make sure that your subject line is as effective as possible. The objective can be part of your subject line. For example, if you need information about the Smith account, the subject line could be: Requesting Information about the Smith Account. When the recipient opens the inbox and sees the subject line, he or she knows immediately what the email is about and what you're asking for. Do not use generic subject lines such as: Need Information or Request or Follow-up as it is very difficult in the future for someone to find a particular email because the subject line is too vague and general. Efficiency will be greatly increased if you're as clear as possible when you cite the objective in the subject line.

Tip 4: Start at the beginning. As when writing a handwritten letter, begin your email with some sort of polite salutation such as Dear Fred or Hello Fred or Hi Fred. As a word of caution, in your salutation don't be too casual. Don't write, "Yo" or "Hey." You can use those greetings in your personal emails, but never at work. After the salutation, write a brief introduction as to the purpose of your email. For example, if you are writing about a particular project, you could say, "The purpose of this email is for me to learn more about the Sound Wisdom book project." This way you immediately notify the email recipient what you want or need. A simple way to describe this sequence is SIP—**S**alutation, **I**ntroduction, and **P**urpose. It is also nice to include a line something like, "I hope you are doing well and enjoying your summer." This establishes a friendly tone from the outset of the email. I'm not suggesting a long, rambling introduction, just a polite comment to set the tone, briefly.

Tip 5: Bullets. I have always believed that bullet points are easier to read. But this not just my opinion, research has shown that bulleted lists in emails are more effective and more readable. According to research by the Nielsen Norman Group, people look at list with bullets more often than a list without bullets: 70 percent versus 55 percent. There are several other advantages: 1) bullets make an email easier to read; 2) they make your separate points clearer; 3) easier to cut and paste your email into their reply and answer each point individually; 4) helps you think more clearly about the points that you want to make.

Tip 6: Leave the drama on the stage. Because email is a tool for business communication, emotion should not be part of an email. You may know of workplace examples of emails sent in anger. Then the receiver of the email responded with an angry response, which led to an email war. This does not serve any purpose and can risk careers. It is unprofessional, uncalled for, and in today's work environment could even be considered a form of harassment. As Judith Martin said, "We are now seeing email that people thought they had deleted showing up as evidence in court."

You can't erase email. Emails should never be thought of as confidential. Employers have a legal right to access your email, so always think of your email as public. Never send anything in an email that you would not want repeated or forwarded. As that fact becomes more commonly realized, people will be a little wiser about what they type. Here is a good guideline that you may want to follow. If someone seems to be upset in an email, do not respond in kind or respond to the email—actually pick up the phone and call the person. If you are in the same building, go see them face to face. This will give you credibility and increase your communication skills by not responding to any email drama.

Tip 7: I say potato you say potato. One of the problems with email—it is massively open to interpretation. In many cases, a person who sends an email (the sender) sends an email with a certain intent. Unfortunately, oftentimes the person who receives the email (the receiver) interprets the message in a different way from the sender's intent. Why does this happen? Everybody sees the world through their own original lens based on their experiences and background. When someone misinterprets an email and they communicate with you their misinterpretation, you may want to respond to clarify, or pick up the phone, or go see the receiver in person. Clarify. Communicate. Calmly.

Tip 8: No emojis in business email. Many people working in corporate America like to use emoticons and the world-famous "smiley face." Unfortunately, this is very unprofessional. Think of it this way, would you want an email filled with emojis to be read by your CEO or a board member of your corporation? The answer is probably no. Feel free to use emoticons when you're emailing your friends if you so choose, but avoid using them at work because it can affect your image in a negative way. Don't take my word for it. In a study published in *Social Psychological and Personality Science,* researchers found the people who use emoticons emails are viewed as being less competent. Using three different experiments with 549 participants from twenty-nine different countries, the researchers found that even though emoticons have a positive effect on the tone of the message, the effect was often outweighed by the decrease in perception of competence. Isn't that amazing how a small symbol can affect how someone else perceives you? Beyond that, researchers discovered that the use of emoticons also affected the willingness of email recipients to share information, making it more difficult for them to work together. I have received emails from people where at the bottom of the email, just below the signature line, there was an animated emoticon jumping around blinking at me. It is distracting.

Tip 9: It is a colorful world, but the pallet should not extend to email. Every now and then I receive an email that is a colorful masterpiece. There is one color for the bullets, a different color for the wording, a different color for the heading. This is first of all extremely time-consuming and second of all makes people wonder how you had so much time to color code all of the different elements of your email.

It's also distracting. I love color, but it should not be part of your email. Stick to one color—black.

Tip 10: FYI on the CC and BCC. We meet many people in the corporate world who are driven *crazy* by people hitting "reply all" and then everyone has to read the answer. When you compose an email, be aware of who you are designating as a CC and BCC. You don't have to copy everyone in the world; in fact, we find that most people copy way too many people. Many executives we speak to say that they are weary because everyone copies everyone in every email. Use CC and BCC sparingly; also keep in mind BCC can be forwarded to other people who you didn't want to see that message.

Tip 11: Follow the mom rules. Growing up, your parents may have taught you to say please and thank you. The same rules apply when composing an email. Use polite terms like "thank you" and "please" and "you're welcome." For example, write, "Please answer Mr. Jones as soon as possible" rather than "Answer Mr. Jones immediately." You will receive a much better response. One sounds like an order, the other like a request. It really is all about tone; and in an email, people can't hear your vocal tone, they only have words to interpret your meaning. So people make assumptions about your tone based on the words you select.

Tip 12: Your signature. Every email you send should contain your signature block. This is very easy to do because it can be set up automatically to appear at the end of every email you send. The signature block is valuable information for the receiver. I can't tell you how many times we get emails from people who at the end of the email write, Sincerely, Joe. This is very frustrating because the signature block is missing a lot of valuable information. Keep in mind that your signature block is a form of customer service, providing information that the receiver would have to look up. Your signature block should contain your full name, title, company name, website, physical address, email address, and phone number. I have always been a fan of motivation and motivational books; however, sometimes people use their signature block as a motivational seminar! Some emails we receive have a signature block that includes six or seven motivational quotes and several website addresses. In theory it is a good idea, but in practice it delivers a perception of being a little unprofessional. My advice is to limit it to one motivational quote.

Tip 13: Check, please. An essential part of email communication is to make sure that your email is free from misspellings and errors. Let's face it, errors affect how people perceive you. Research from a Grammarly study indicates that 67 percent of the people who responded thought that typos in emails at work were "uncalled for." Before sending an email, make sure to read through it carefully looking for misspellings and word omissions. Sometimes people write a sentence and accidentally leave out a word. Also, note that spell check often does not differentiate between words such as *form or from* depending on the context. Take the time to read back through each line of your email to look for misspellings and other errors. Also look for grammatical errors. If grammar is not one of your strong suits, have a colleague review your email or use an online research tool like Grammarly.

Tip 14: Privacy? The mistake people often make is that email is private and confidential. The reality is: everyone you send an email to has the ability to press one button and forward your email to anyone in the world. One of our clients (who shall go nameless for obvious reasons) worked for a governmental agency and sent an email of a confidential nature. Unfortunately, within five days that email was forwarded to a member of the press and ended up being prominently featured as a headline story in a major city newspaper. A good rule of thumb for email is not to email anything you are not willing to put on a postcard or post in the employee lunchroom. Human beings are flawed; it's just too easy for them to occasionally forward an email to someone they know and asked them to keep it a secret, which never happens. Also keep in mind in an era when people tend to be very litigious, email can be printed and presented as evidence at trial. Email is always public domain—even if you don't think it is.

Tip 15: Finished? Close your emails the same way you open, with some sort of salutation. For example, you write, "Thank you for your time" or "All my best" or "Have a great day." Close with some sort of business sign off such as "Sincerely, Rachael" or "Respectfully, Rachael Doyle" or "Regards, Rachael."

Tip 16: I'm waiting. Always reply in a timely manner. I am often very surprised people in the workplace receive an email and then *never respond*. When asked about their lack of response people say, "I'm busy." Who isn't busy? A good rule of thumb is to answer every email within 24 hours, and if you can't respond within 24 hours with an answer, at least reply that you're aware of the email and you are *working* on the response. Keep in mind that if you don't respond, you will get more emails asking for responses, which adds to your workload. Not responding to email is like standing beside someone who asking you a question and ignoring them instead of answering. It is disrespectful and rude.

Tip 17: The name game. One of the most important words in the English language is someone's name. So please, please, please cross check and double check to make sure you're spelling people's first and last names correctly when you send an email. It sounds very simplistic, but if you misspell someone's name you automatically damage your credibility a bit. As you know, my name is Rachael, which is spelled Rach**A**el; but most often I receive emails with the salutation Dear Rach**E**l. Starting off by misspelling someone's name does not make the best impression. My husband's name is *Shawn*, and you can imagine the myriad of different ways people spell his name in emails (Shaun, Sean, Chon) despite the fact they just received an email from him or have his business card or have met him in person! A great way to connect with people is to say and spell their names correctly. Details really do matter—it's very personal.

The bottom line is, email is only one form of communication at work. Make sure all your communication is as effective and efficient as possible.

"What's in a name? That which we call a rose by any other name would smell as sweet."
—WILLIAM SHAKESPEARE

The Phone and Voicemail

"That's the great thing about a tractor, you can't really hear the phone ring."
—JEFF FOXWORTHY

In our company, we offer a communication program called *The Leader Within* where we train people to communicate in meetings and presentations, verbally and in writing. It's amazing how by improving these skills your communication can be transformational.

One form of important communication and connection is the telephone. These days people usually have a phone at home, at our work desk, and a personal cell phone. Cell phones are a blessing and a curse. The good news is we can be reached almost anywhere at any time. The bad news is we can be reached almost anywhere at any time. Phones are a great connection to information, entertainment, communication, and family and friends.

Think of all forms of communication—phone, email, texts, meetings, etc.—as different channels, each having its own strengths and liabilities. The following are some interesting statistics about phones and voicemail:

- In a recent campaign to cut costs at the company, both J.P. Morgan and Coca-Cola asked employees if they were willing to eliminate their voicemail on their office phone. At J.P. Morgan, 65 percent of the people eliminated office voicemail, which saved the company $3 million annually. At Coca-Cola, only 6 percent of employees decided to keep their office voicemail. To be clear, these were all people who were not in customer service.

- New research conducted by British psychologists show that young adults use their smart phones roughly twice as much as they estimated. They found that young adults use their phone an average of five hours a day, one-third of their total waking hours.

■ New research shows that the average person checks his or her cell phone every twelve minutes which equals eighty times a day.

USING YOUR PHONE EFFECTIVELY

The first area we need to cover is using the phone effectively. These ideas apply to using your desk phone in your office or using a mobile device. The phone is a great tool to connect and communicate with people.

Tip 1: Answer please and smile. According to research, as much as 80 percent of business calls go to voicemail. Isn't that number shocking? You've probably had this experience—you call a number expecting to talk to someone but the person is unavailable. You leave a voicemail and then await a return call. Many times it ends up being a game of phone tag that you play all day long. When you're at your desk, answer the phone if possible; but more importantly, be aware of *the way* you answer the phone. There are four important elements to answering the phone efficiently and effectively: 1) answer by the third ring; 2) have a pleasant greeting; 3) speak with a tone that says you love your work; 4) say who you are and your position. For example, "Hello, this is Rachael in the engineering department, how may help you?" The person calling now knows they reached Rachael and more importantly they know that they have the right department. With a clear and not rushed vocal tone, let the caller know that you're glad to be where you are.

Smile! Your smile projects over the phone. I often call companies and organizations where the person who answers the phone just says hello, not sounding very excited to be at work— sometimes the person even sounds comatose! Remember, the way you answer the phone is an important part of your company brand. Some trainees say they're not worried about the brand or how they answer the phone because they are not in customer service. Our response is that *everyone* is in customer service; you are either serving external customers or you're serving internal customers. Besides, let's face it, everyone who calls wants a pleasant person on the other end of the line. Talking on the phone is simply radio not television, so the tone of your voice is critically important, as it is the *only* connection people have to rely on. Research has shown that when people smile when talking on the phone it actually changes their vocal tone and they sound more pleasant. In many call centers around the world, companies place small mirrors in front of the customer service representatives to remind them that they should be smiling. Nobody wants to call a company and be greeted by Mr. Grumpy Pants. Be kind and friendly and make the callers want to do business with you.

Tip 2: Action, take one. I'm often amazed how often I call a company and the person answering the phone is in the middle of doing something else. They may be engaged in a conversation with another person or typing an email—I can hear the keys clattering in the background. When you answer the phone, stop everything else and focus on the person who has called. Try to rule out as much background noise as possible. Also be cautious of your voice volume in an open office environment.

Tip 3: The name game. When calling, first state your name to let them know who is calling. For example, you may say, "Hello, this is Susie calling from the Motivation store, and your name is?" When you give your name first, the other person knows who you are and knows from where you're calling. When you get the person's name, say it throughout the call. This guideline applies whether you are making a call inside your company or outside of your company. Using someone's name is a great way to establish a connection—people like hearing their own name, but don't overdo it.

Tip 4: Permission, please. When someone answers the phone, the person may or may not be expecting your call. After your initial greeting, ask the other person if now is a convenient time to chat. Keep in mind you may have caught the person off guard. It is a courtesy to ask for the person's time. Maybe you will be asked to call back at a time that is more convenient. Also keep in mind if the person is in the middle of something, the communication is probably not going to be very effective because of the distraction. It may be better to talk when you can have his or her undivided attention.

Tip 5: May I have your attention, please. According to research by the Cleveland Clinic, only 2.5 percent of people are able to multitask effectively. If you are talking to someone on the phone while you are checking emails or text messages, straightening your desk, or filing, you're not giving the other person your undivided attention and you're going to miss hearing important information. Besides, I think we can agree that most times when we are talking to someone on the phone and the person is doing something else, we can tell they are distracted. I know that you're very busy at work, but believe it or not, you are actually being more productive and more effective if you don't multitask when talking on the phone. A recent study by Stanford University indicates that multitasking can cause a loss of 40 percent of your productivity! And believe me, if I can hear the keyboard tapping in the background—so can everyone else. If you have to look something up during the call, say to the other person, "Let me go ahead and look that up while we're speaking in order to give you an answer." This way you're telling the other person that you are temporarily distracted from the conversation, which is a courtesy. Another way to ensure that you are paying close attention when you're on a call with someone is to actually take notes so you can recall what was said later on.

Tip 6: Speak to me. If there is a very clear reason why you need to put the caller on speakerphone, then do so. But before you do, there are two vital rules. It is critically important to: 1) ask the person if you have their permission to turn on the speaker so that others in the room can hear the conversation and the reason why you need to do so; 2) tell the person who else is present in the room; this is a courtesy to all parties involved in the call. If you work in an open office environment, or even a cube style environment, be very careful about putting people on speaker because it becomes an enormous distraction for others working around you. You may want to instead go to a conference room before putting the conversation on speaker. The same rules also apply if you're using Skype or some other Internet technology where you will be able to see them and have them on speaker. It's best to use a conference room.

Tip 7: Hold on a moment. If you are on a call with someone, whether an internal customer or an extra customer, and you have to put the person on hold, ask for permission first, and *wait for the answer*. If you have to place someone on hold, also explain the reason why. When the person agrees to be put on hold, make sure not to keep them waiting for more than two or three minutes, at most. When you return to the call, thank the person for holding. Say something like, "Okay, Jim, I have the information you are looking for. Thank you so much for holding." If you have to leave someone on hold more than two to three minutes, let them know that it's going to take longer than you anticipated and you would be happy to call them back. Everyone has had the infuriating experience of calling somewhere and being put on hold without permission.

Tip 8: Snack attack. A good guideline to follow when talking to anyone on the phone is to not eat any food or chew anything. This includes snacks, your lunch, or chewing gum. You may think they can't tell you are eating, but they can— and it gives the impression that you care more about what you're eating than talking to the person on the other end of the phone.

Tip 9: Wrap it up, I'll take it. At the end of the phone call when the discussion has concluded, make sure to wrap up the call with two very important final comments:1) make sure you agree on what each person is committing to by summarizing what everyone agreed to do; 2) thank the person(s) for their time, telling them something positive at the end of the call so you end on a positive note. For example, say, "In summary, John and Susan will be researching the statistics for the project. Mary and Sam are going to contact the engineering department and pull the numbers we need. Thank you all for the good, productive conversation. Have a great afternoon."

VOICEMAIL TIPS

Tip 1: First impression, last impression. The first thing to think about in terms of voicemail, is what people will hear when they call you and you're not available. First, your voicemail needs to be positive and sound like you are happy to be at work—someone they want to do business with. Once you have recorded your voicemail, play it back and listen to make sure you sound positive, upbeat, and energetic. Keep your message short with a greeting and give instructions about how to leave a voicemail for you. For example, you might say, "Hello, this is Rachael and your call is very important to me. Please leave me a message, the purpose of your call, and the best time to return your call. I will be happy to get back to you as soon as possible. Have a great day." This is just a suggestion. Make the voicemail your own; but if you use these key elements, you will have a very successful voicemail in terms of getting results. As author and speaker Jeffrey Gitomer said, "The voicemail that you record on your phone is the impression of who you are when you are not there. It informs the caller how original you are, how creative you are, and how friendly you are."

Tip 2: Voicemail etiquette. Leaving a voicemail is an art form in itself. When you make a call, be prepared if the person is not available. When you hear a voicemail message, leave your name, your company name, the reason for your call, and most importantly your phone number said slowly enough for someone to actually write down the number. Before saying your number, say "my number is..." and pause, then say your number slowly. Leave your phone number at the beginning of the call and at the end of the call, which gives the person two opportunities to write it down. I am quite amazed at how many people from many organizations leave me messages and either don't leave their complete name and why they are calling, or say their phone number so fast it sets a new land speed record. Then I have to listen to the voicemail repeatedly in order to catch all of the numbers. Slow down there race car driver, particularly when stating your phone number!

CELL PHONE GUIDELINES

Even though the general phone guidelines apply, there some specific ideas about cell phones that you may want to consider. Here are some ideas and tips about cell phones:

Tip 1: Out of plain sight. We often find it amusing that during training programs people will come into the room, sit down, and place on the table in front of them three devices: a work cell phone, a personal cell phone, and some sort of other device such as an iPad or laptop. One suggestion: whenever you're in meetings at work, keep your phones out of sight and most importantly silence each one out of courtesy for the rest of the group. The only exceptions are when you have training programs that require interaction from your cell phone or laptop. One of our clients in South Florida demands that whenever anyone is attending a live training, they surrender their phones in the front of the room into a specially selected bag that is marked with their name. They are only allowed to look at their cell phones during the break. The reason for this is people were continually looking at their cell phones checking messages and sending text messages during training. We jokingly called the bags in the front of the room the Apple daycare center!

Tip 2: No text, no problem. When you are meeting with someone, actually make an effort not to text on your phone—it is considered to be rude in almost every culture. It sends a signal that what the person is saying is less important than what you are reading or accessing on your phone. Plus, you miss parts of each.

Tip 3: Step out to step up. If you must answer a personal call on your cell phone and you are meeting with someone, simply say, "Excuse me one moment," and step out of the room into a private location where you can talk. Conversely, if you're meeting with someone in their office and the person has to accept a phone call, ask if you should to step out of the room to give the person privacy.

Tip 4: Words have power. When you are on the phone, don't get upset, don't curse, or use any profanity. You stand a chance of offending the person you called, offending anyone who can hear you, and of possibly damaging your reputation and credibility.

Tip 5: Speaker of the house. If you have to take a call or you have to listen to a voicemail when other people are around, under no circumstances should you put the caller on speakerphone. Listening to voicemails on speaker is rude to all the other people around you. It is important to be aware of your surroundings and how your activities can affect others by being either distracting, or worse, be perceived as rude. Another point many don't think about, other people feel like they're intruding on your privacy when they have to hear your voicemail messages or your private conversations. We often travel on business and are amazed how often people on planes and trains check their voicemails on speaker or have very loud personal conversations that can be heard by people sitting several rows in front and behind them before takeoff. I believe in sharing, but not that much! When talking in public, keep it short and low volume.

Tip 6: Ring the bell. I was once boarding a plane for a business trip, and the person in front of me had a cell phone that started ringing. Unfortunately, the ring tone was an angry cat yowling and screaming. I was quite confused and puzzled as to why someone would actually *choose* that ringtone. Let's face it, in the corporate world everything is about perception, so think about the ringtone you select for your phone. Make sure it delivers the most positive impression possible. If your ringtone is a hard rock song or rap or "Shake Your Booty" by KC and the Sunshine Band, that is fun and fine, but how will other people perceive you if your phone accidentally rings in the middle of an important meeting? You may become the butt of their jokes, or worse.

Tip 7: Keeping it real. One general rule to is follow is it you are talking about a health issue, personal issue, professional problem, or financial issues don't talk about it publicly on your cell phone where people around can hear you—it is embarrassing and unprofessional. Remember, private conversations should be just that—*private!*

Tip 8: Lights, camera, action. Always remember that almost everyone has a phone that is also a camera and a video recorder. Anyone can record anyone anytime—that means anyone can take your picture or text or record you at any time. The point is, you are always on stage when you are at work whether you know it or not.

Tip 9: Sorry, I lost you. If for some reason you get disconnected, call the person back. If you don't reach the person, leave a message.

Tip 10: Texting is a tool. When texting, keep in mind the guidelines I have already outlined for general courtesy. Beyond that, the following are a few things to keep in mind when texting:

- Be nice; some hide behind the safety of a text and will write things they wouldn't say face to face. Just don't.

- Be brief; text messages should be short and sweet. If longer, pick up the phone and call.

- Be aware of time. Don't text someone late at night or too early in the morning, it may disturb or wake them up.

- Check the recipient before you hit send. You don't want to send the flirty message intended for your spouse to your boss.

- Texting is permanent. When you send a text, you can't correct mistakes or pull it back.

- Keep it professional at all times. Use proper language and don't resort to slang or web words like LOL (laugh out loud) or BRB (be right back).

- If you text to multiple people, remember all replies go to all people!
- Tone in a text can be misinterpreted, so be careful and concise.

Let's face it, phones are tools like any other tool at work. We have to think about them and figure out how to use them most effectively and strategically. You can do this!

I believe it is important today to have a balance. Many have our cell phones on from the moment we get up until we go to sleep. Many people place the phone near them at night and use it to wake up. I think you should use an alarm clock and put the phone away at night in another room. Technology can be addictive—it is up to us to find a good balance in our lives. We need to take time to look up every great once and awhile and see the world and people around us.

"Technology can be our best friend, and technology can also be the biggest party pooper of our lives. It interrupts our own story, interrupts our ability to have a thought or a daydream, to imagine something wonderful, because we're too busy bridging the walk from the cafeteria back to the office on the cell phone."
—STEVEN SPIELBERG

Effective Meetings

"If you had to identify, in one word, the reason why the human race has not achieved, and never will achieve, its full potential, that word would be 'meetings.'"
—DAVE BARRY

It seems like the bane of people's existence at work is meetings, meetings, and more bloody meetings! Most people when asked if they would like to attend a meeting, would rather do anything else! Mop floors, drive bamboo shoots under their fingernails, sort laundry, or sort junk mail. Yet if you think about it, meetings are a great way to connect, communicate, and really get results! If you do them right.

According to Inc. and the online meeting company Fuze, here are some staggering meeting statistics to ponder:

- There are 25 million meetings per day in the United States—per day!

- More than $37 billion per year is spent on unproductive meetings.

- Fifteen percent of an organization's collective time is spent in meetings.

- Middle managers spend 35 percent of their time in meetings.

- Upper management spends 50 percent of their time in meetings.

- People spend up to four hours per week preparing for status update meetings.

- Most meetings are unproductive. In fact, executives consider more than 67 percent of meetings as failures.

What can you do to make these meeting statistics better? There is good news! There are lots of ways to make your meeting more productive.

Tip 1: I object. To have effective meetings, determine the objective of the meeting first. For example, you may have a team who needs to brainstorm a new product, or solve an engineering problem, or evaluate vendors, or provide an update on projects. Whatever the issue, have a specific objective for each meeting. That way the meeting will have more focus, will be more disciplined in the approach, and people will not be wasting their time, energy, and effort.

At the beginning of the meeting, clearly articulate the objective so that everyone is on the same page. In our company, we spent a lot of time training people how to have effective meetings and how to communicate and connect with people on a daily basis. One comment we often hear from many people is that they don't know why they are in a meeting or what the meeting is for. You should only invite people who are necessary to meet the objective. Don't invite people who don't need to be there. If they are indirectly involved, provide them meeting notes after the fact, and respect them by not tying up their time.

Tip 2: Could I have a map please? Every meeting should have an agenda citing the objective. A meeting without an agenda can waste a lot of time, effort, and energy. I know this sounds like such a simple suggestion and it is so very obvious. But here is what is interesting. In about 90 percent of the training programs our company facilitates about meetings, at the end of the program, people say their action plan is to start using an agenda. They know they need it, but they don't have one.

Have an agenda in writing, give everybody a copy in advance, and ask the facilitator to use and follow the agenda. The agenda is the track to run on. Many meetings get off track and get derailed because there is no agenda to follow. Too many meetings end up with discussions that were not part of the agenda. That drives people crazy and wastes time. An agenda has many benefits:

- An agenda increases focus.
- It is a visual record for later reference.
- The agenda can be used to redirect people who get off track.
- It can be used as a timing device so your meeting does not get too lengthy.

An agenda is a simple planning and preparation tool. As Seneca said, "Luck is a matter of preparation meeting opportunity."

Tip 3: Power to the people. When planning a meeting, think very carefully about who should be in the meeting and who could make significant contributions to the effectiveness of the meeting itself. If you can explain why you feel they are needed and what contributions they can make, they will feel valued and appreciated. Clarify what you think their roles will be.

Tip 4: Rock and role. You may have heard of Toastmasters. Toastmasters helps people develop better communication skills and also how to effectively lead meetings. If you attend a Toastmasters meeting, one thing is clear— the role that each person plays in the meeting. Each person has a specifically designed role. For your next meeting, think about what role you want each person to play, one person can be the facilitator, another person can be the note taker, someone can make sure that the agenda is on track, another can be the timer, well you get the idea. If you can clearly identify the roles that each person plays in the meeting, the meeting will be much more effective and people will feel more appreciated. Another great technique is to ask people to volunteer for roles, explain the various roles available and ask who would like to do each.

Tip 5: Time after time. All meetings should start and end on time. Too many meetings start late, creating havoc with people's schedules. It's kind of like the doctors' office— you arrive early to fill out all the forms, and then sit in the lobby and then in the little room they take you to, and then the doctor is never on time! Don't have your meetings be like a doctor's office! The person who organizes the meeting, or the facilitator, should manage the time so the meeting starts and ends on time. Always arrive at your meetings on time.

Tip 6: Guide me. I think every meeting should have some agreed-on *guidelines* about how the meeting will be run and how people will operate in the meeting. Ask the group to develop guidelines and stick by them. These will improve communication, increase connection, and increase focus. Examples of guidelines could include:

- Silence cell phones.
- No side conversations.
- Facilitator is in charge of the meeting.

- Stick to the agenda.
- If there is an emergency or urgent call, take it outside.
- No texting during the meeting.
- No coming in and out during the meeting.
- Treat everyone with respect.
- Talk to one person at a time.
- No interrupting.
- Ask questions.

Tip 7:   Take a seat. One area to consider for improved communication and connection in a meeting is where people sit. Maybe you have heard of the term "proxemics." Proxemics is the relationship of people in space. If you want to connect with people, you need to be aware of proxemics barriers. If you meet with someone and you have a desk or table between you, that is a *proxemic and psychological* barrier. So the best approach is to sit beside the person which gets people to relax and connect more. In meetings, ask people to sit in certain spots. If you are meeting with a supplier or vendor or partner, don't have their people sit on one side of the table and your team on the other—mix up the seating.

Tip 8:   A name is but a name. Right? One of the most valuable words in the human language is someone's name. The reason I bring this up again is when in a meeting where people don't know each other, go around the room quickly and introduce everyone briefly. Ask people to write their names on the table tents in front of them. If you don't have any, one piece of white copy paper folded makes an excellent table tent. Call on people by name, use their name. This also makes it easier for the people attending the meeting to recognize and remember names.

Tip 9: Host with the most. Whoever is hosting or chairing the meeting is the host. The host should make sure: 1) that people feel comfortable and welcome; 2) there is a place to hang up coats, scarfs, or umbrellas; 3) everyone is offered coffee or water or pointed to where they can get it; 4) that everyone knows where the exits are and how to get to the restrooms. It is the same as if you are hosting people in your home, the same rules apply in your office space. Yes, this is true no matter if the people are internal or external meeting attendees. The only exception is if everyone there is in the same department and they already know where everything is and what to do.

Tip 10: Change it up. Every now and then it may be a good idea to vary regularly occurring meetings by choosing a different place or different time to make it more interesting. As Tom Hodgkinson said, "Meetings, clearly, can take place anywhere, and wouldn't it be nice to see your coworkers lounging on the grass with their shoes off?" Perhaps you don't have to go that far, but you should be creative. Think about having your meeting in a different room, a different place, a different time, or over lunch. This can make meetings fresh again.

Tip 11: On a clear day I can see forever. We have seen many great meeting rooms around the world, which on the surface seem great. But there is usually a problem—the rooms are engineered for distraction! Many rooms have several clear walls with amazing views of a city or the ocean or a golf course. Whoever designed it thought it was a great idea, but the sights become very distracting. If you can, arrange seating so that people have their backs to the distractions if at all possible.

Tip 12: Park it here. Another technique that can be very helpful is using a white board or chart as a "parking lot." A parking lot is a useful device used to record items not on the agenda or are off topic. This allows you to go back to the original agenda but also acknowledge the person who brought up the idea, making sure the idea doesn't get "lost." It can be a great tool, and we have seen it used very effectively many times. The person facilitating says, "Okay, thanks Jim, that is a great idea, but something we aren't covering today. To make sure we don't lose it, let's write it on the parking lot list."

Tip 13: Do you follow? Another very effective tool is that after the meeting someone sends out a brief summary to everyone who attended. The follow-up should be executive summary style and no more than a few pages. There is an important reason to do this—the "forgetting curve." Research on the forgetting curve shows that within one hour, people will have forgotten an average of 50 percent of the information you presented. Within 24 hours, they have forgotten an average of 70 percent of new information; and within a week, forgetting claims an average of 90 percent. So a follow-up email gives us a chance to remind people of what was discussed. Plus one other thought is that people often go from your meeting into another meeting immediately. So follow-up is essential.

Tip 14: Are you engaged? I'm not talking about your relationship status. It is very important to keep people engaged. There are many ways to do that: 1) Ask the facilitator to get people involved; 2) Have a lengthy questions and answers list 3) Divide people into small groups and then ask them to report their ideas and conclusions; 4) Ask people in the beginning to participate and be active. Many perspective clients for our training programs often ask us if the training is "engaging." We tell them it is, because they don't have a choice! Design a meeting that encourages engagement. When people are engaged, they are not bored, they want to contribute. When people are asked for their input, they feel appreciated and valued.

Tip 15: Break it. Far too many meetings go very long and don't have breaks. This leads to fatigue and less effective meetings. Most research shows that breaks need to happen every 50 to 90 minutes. After a break, people return fresher and able to do more. Researchers from the University of Illinois at Urbana-Champaign studied four groups of people. Each group worked on a brain-intensive task for 50 minutes. The group that took more breaks had the highest mental stamina at the end of the 50 minutes. If planning a meeting, plan breaks. You will find people will appreciate it. There is also another advantage of breaks, people talk with each other on the break and connect on a social and business level. One other tip—announce the break and announce when it is starting and ending. When time is up, start.

Tip 16: Table that. The way tables are arranged can have a big impact on your meeting. Based on our company conducting training for more than 30 years, the following table setups are the best choices (in order): Please see diagram.

1. U Shape. Tables are set up in a U shape with the opening facing the facilitator. The great thing about this table arrangement is when there are discussions, everyone can see everyone else. The facilitator can also walk around inside the U.

2. Pods. Tables are set in pods that seat about four to six people per group and are spread around the room. All chairs are facing the front of the room. This allows people to interact at their tables and they are already in groups, or as we call it, "groupified"!

3. Rounds. The same as pods, but with round tables, and only half of each table has seats. These are also sometimes called "half rounds." The advantages are the same as pods.

4. Conference room table. A giant table that can't be moved that everyone sits around causes a problem when there are more people than can sit at the table. Extra people have

to sit at the "outside ring" against the walls and they can feel disconnected from the inner ring of people at the table.

5. Classroom style. Tables are arranged in rows with each person having their back to the row behind them. This is the worst setup because when people talk, they can't be seen by those sitting behind them.

Think carefully about table and chair setup.

Tip 17: Work it. Before any meeting, if there is anything you want the meeting attendees to review, study, evaluate, or give ideas and opinions, send it to them in advance so they can review it. It is not fair to spring a new subject at people on the spot and ask for opinions. Give them the courtesy of looking at it in advance.

I know many of these tips sound like simple ideas and they are; but if they are so simple, why don't most people do them? Connect and communicate—before, during, and after your meetings.

Arianna Huffington, cofounder of *Huffington Post* website, said, "If we have a clear agenda in advance and we are fully present and fully contributing, the meetings do go much faster."

A LINKEDIN PROFILE
PICTURE YOU SHOULD
NOT USE...

UNLESS YOU REALLY
ARE A DOG

CHAPTER 6

LinkedIn and Twitter Networking

"Active participation on LinkedIn is the best way to say, 'Look at me!' without saying 'Look at me!'"
—BOBBY DARNELL

Networking is very important for connecting with others to promote your business, gain information about your career, find employees, etc. You can network with LinkedIn or Twitter.

LINKEDIN

Let's talk about LinkedIn first. Our company has had great success with LinkedIn as a marketing and connection tool. Think of LinkedIn as Facebook for business. Here are some very interesting facts about LinkedIn:

- It is the world's largest professional network with more than 562 million users in more than 200 countries and territories worldwide.

- LinkedIn's monthly active user base reached 260 million in March 2017.

- Sixty-one million LinkedIn users are senior level influencers and 40 million are in decision-making positions.

- LinkedIn is the most-used social media platform among Fortune 500 companies.

The following are some tips, techniques, and ideas about this remarkable tool for connecting with other people.

Tip 1: Profile here, please. On LinkedIn you can create a profile once you set up your LinkedIn account. It can be a lot of work, but it is a great marketing document and build your credibility as well as make a great impression on people who connect to you. Explain clearly what you do in your profile. Many times when I'm talking to a potential client about Shawn Doyle (founder of our company) working with them, they say, "We have already read through Shawn's profile on LinkedIn and his credentials are very impressive." If you have a really strong profile, it makes you easier to find on Google. Follow LinkedIn's instructions and fill out your profile completely—100 percent! Many recruiters use LinkedIn to find potential employees, so it's a great way to be found. As LinkedIn expert Melanie Pinola said, "One of the great things about LinkedIn is it isn't the same kind of networking that happens at conventions, where you're wearing a name tag, trying to meet strangers, and awkwardly attempting to make small talk. LinkedIn is networking without the pressure."

Tip 2: Say cheese. If you set up a LinkedIn profile and you do not include a photo, they place an avatar where your picture should be. It looks like a robot's head. Since you're not a robot, don't do that to yourself. People want to see who they are connecting with. Let everyone see your warm smile, your sparkle, and best professional face! One important tip: have a professional picture taken by a professional, it makes all the difference in the world. We see too many pictures on LinkedIn that make a horrible first impression. This is *your brand* so make sure you show yourself in the best light. We see people whose photos are:

- A blurry, out-of-focus picture.

- A cartoon of themselves—unless you are cartoonist, bad idea. Even then people want to see the cartoonist's face.

- Of ten people all standing in a group and we have to guess which one is the LinkedIn person. (Don't make me guess.)

- With someone else—girlfriend, boyfriend, husband, wife, partner. I can kind of guess, but it's very unprofessional. Also these photos can often be in the wrong setting like Mardi Gras, on the beach, or in a bar.

- Too revealing or inappropriate. If the picture makes people wonder, "What the heck?" it is not good. Don't wear anything in your picture you wouldn't wear at work, including the picture of you in mouse ears at a Disney park.

- Pets as their profile picture, including a crossed-eyed German Shepherd. Yes, I have actually seen this and I wish it wasn't true!

Tip 3: Invitation, please. After you join LinkedIn, you can invite everyone who is in your address book to link to you. Once they accept, they are part of your network and considered a direct connection. Some people have just a few hundred connections, some have thousands. The CEO of our company has 24,545 direct connections! This can be controversial because people often wonder if they should link to everyone? It's up to you, but I would say yes, unless it is someone you object to on a personal level, or in a profession that you don't want to connect with. But overall the idea is to build your network so you can get to know more people and new people. If you link just to people you actually know, your network will be very small. The idea is to expand your network and connect with more people in all aspects of business. You may also want to connect to some in order to help them connect to other businesses.

Tip 4: Gee, thanks. When someone accepts your invite or you accept theirs, they are now part of your network, so thank the person. Send a short message on LinkedIn; you can send a direct message to a connection. You should: 1) thank them; 2) offer something you have in common such as, "I noticed you grew up in West Virginia, so did I!"; 3) ask if there is any way you can help; 4) invite the person to join other groups you are part of on LinkedIn; 5) refer to one of your contacts; 6) invite him or her to join your group if you have one; 7) invite the person to join any associations you belong to that may be beneficial. People appreciate being appreciated. In this initial communication, don't try to sell or market the person on any service or product, just connect. If you don't have the time or bandwidth to do this, you can hire a virtual assistant to do it for you each month.

Tip 5: Hot off the press. An interesting feature of LinkedIn is to publish articles that you write. You can write an article on your area of expertise and then publish it on LinkedIn. Here is how LinkedIn describes it:

> *We're always looking for new ways for members to contribute professional insights on LinkedIn. Our publishing platform allows members, in addition to Influencers, to publish articles about their*

expertise and interests. While publishing an article doesn't mean you're a LinkedIn Influencer, it does allow you to further establish your professional identity by expressing your opinions and sharing your experiences.

When you publish an article:

- Your original content becomes part of your professional profile. It is displayed in the Articles section of your LinkedIn profile.

- It's shared with your connections and followers in their news feeds, and sometimes through notifications.

- Members who aren't in your network can follow you from your article, so your next article will be surfaced in their feeds.

You don't need approval from an editor, just publish your article! But make sure that it is well written by using some sort of editing tool (I like Grammarly) or a human editor to clean up your writing—you want to make sure it is great. Let's say you are a CPA. You can write an article about the six biggest mistakes businesses make when working with an accounting firm. You can publish that article on LinkedIn and then share it on social media, on your webpage, and in a newsletter, just to name a few ideas. There is also an additional hidden benefit for publishing articles on LinkedIn that many people never consider. Each time you publish an article on LinkedIn, LinkedIn is nice enough to provide for you *analytics* which show how many people read the article, who commented on the article, and who liked the article. This obviously becomes a great opportunity to connect with people who commented on your article or read it or liked it. This is another opportunity to reach out to people who have given a thumbs-up or a positive comment.

Tip 6: I'm in the group. A great feature of LinkedIn is the ability to join groups. What is a group on LinkedIn? Here is how they define it: "LinkedIn Groups are hubs on LinkedIn which provide a place for professionals in the same industry or with similar interests to share content, find answers, post and view jobs, make business contacts, and establish themselves as industry experts." If you're looking for relevant groups to join, simply use the search feature at the top of your home page or select from the suggestions of "Groups you may be interested in." Here are some types of groups you can join:

- Industry groups. For example, we belong to several groups on LinkedIn that are for professional speakers and trainers. If you are in construction, you could search for a group that is construction-industry related. There are some huge industry groups on LinkedIn that have as many as 500,000 members.

- Customer groups. You can join groups that your customers belong to. For example, many of our customers are in Human Resources. So we belong to several of those groups. We also belong to several groups made up of executives. Many of that "category" of our customers are executives.

- Interest groups. Let's say you are interested in reading books. One quick search of groups and you will find there are 2,669 groups on LinkedIn about books. Wow!

One other thing that's important to note, at the time of this writing, LinkedIn allows you to join 100 groups. If you have more than one person in your office or your organization, you can join 200 groups or 300 groups. It's just a matter of how much time you want to invest.

Tip 7: There are rules in this town. Once you have joined a group, it is a good idea to go in and look around at what people are talking about, what people are posting, and what people are saying. I have often said that each group on LinkedIn is like its own sovereign nation, each one has its own rules. One great rule to follow, especially early into your membership in a group, is to not promote your goods and services in a group. It is a good way to get kicked out of the group and never return. What you really want to do is provide value, service, and help to people in the group, then they will perceive you as helpful and a valuable resource.

Tip 8: I have my own tribe. Another fascinating aspect of LinkedIn is the ability to create your own group. At no cost on LinkedIn, you can create a group, give it a name and a logo, and launch it. So imagine being able to create your own group and attract either people in your industry or people who are your highest level responder customers. We have tried this and it has been very successful. We have the largest motivation group on LinkedIn called Motivation Nation with 18,511 members. Each day different members post comments to Motivation Nation and people have many great discussions about how to get and stay motivated. Having your own group also gives you a platform to promote your own products and services to people who want to hear about them because they voluntarily join your group. Having your own group enhances your credibility and makes you a thought leader in your industry or profession.

Tip 9: Just imagine. Once you have joined groups in your industry and groups your customers belong to, then you can go into each group and engage with people in discussions by either: 1) starting a discussion; or 2) answering other people's questions. Keep in mind it's also a great way to identify new connections, because you can then invite people from the group to become a connection of yours. If you are in sales or marketing, it is also a great way to identify potential customers who belong to each respective group. When you are a group member, you can message a group member directly using LinkedIn's InMail system.

Tip 10: Step two. After you have created your own group, when people connect to you, you can invite them to join your group by sending a link. You would write something like, "Hello Sue, thank you for becoming a direct connection. I'm happy to have you as part of my network. I would also like to invite you to join my group IT Executives. Here is the link. This group is intended for people who are interested in being an executive in IT, or are already IT executives." We have found that a very large percentage of people, once they connect to you, are willing to join your group. For example, our CEO has more than 24,000 direct connections, and more than 18,000 people belong to our group Motivation Nation. Admittedly there are some people who are not connected to Shawn who belong to the group; but as the numbers indicate, most of the people do join the group.

Tip 11: The king. There is an old famous saying that "Content is king." That is also true on LinkedIn. One of the keys for success on LinkedIn is to not sell but to provide valuable content and thought leadership. For example, if you belong to group, you can post interesting links to relevant videos for the group (yours or someone else's). You can post relevant news links to stories and information that would be valuable to the group, or links to articles from various websites that people might find interesting or valuable. My point is, you do not necessarily have to always be the creator of the content, you can be the distributor of the content. Finding and posting relevant content gives you credibility as an industry expert.

Tip 12: The list. You have to decide if this is something you want to pursue. There are a number of services that are free or charge a modest fee that will put you on a list of people who are interested in linking with other people. How does this work? Once a month or once a quarter, the service releases names of people who are interested in networking with other people on LinkedIn. After you are on the list, you begin receiving hundreds of invites to link to people on LinkedIn. Our CEO tried this and within two weeks he was getting 100 to 200 invites *a week* from people he did not know. Shawn then realized it was because of the service he had signed up for. To this day he still gets between 200 to 300 invites a week for people wanting to link to him.

Tip 13: The search is on. Another great feature of LinkedIn is the search box at the top of the page. We believe that LinkedIn can be as valuable as Google at times in terms of searches. In the search box you can search for individual people, for companies, or other terms in order to get different results. Let's say I sell supplies to dentists in the northeastern part of the United States. If in the search box I type in "dentist Pennsylvania," I will be shown all the dentists in Pennsylvania with their information and profiles who are Linked in. If I put in the name of a specific dental practice, LinkedIn will show me where the practice is located, how many employees there are, and the employees who belong to the dental practice, as well as their profiles on LinkedIn. This means that LinkedIn becomes a tremendously valuable search tool for finding information, people, and companies. Also, when meeting with someone for the first time, you should look at their profile on LinkedIn before you meet. The profile was written by the person and often contains information that would not normally be publicly available. This also helps you be more prepared by knowing more information about them.

Tip 14: Bam! Many people do not realize that on LinkedIn you have the ability to add media to your profile.

On your profile you could feature a blog that you wrote, a video that you shot talking about who you are and what you do, the video of any media appearances, PowerPoint presentations, audio clips, and any other media you think would enhance your credibility and authority.

Tip 15: Oh, look! Another fascinating aspect of LinkedIn is that it shows you who looked at your profile. If you see in your reports someone on LinkedIn looked at your profile, turn around and invite the person to link to you because interest has already been shown.

Tip 16: Check, please. Make sure to schedule and check your LinkedIn messages consistently—you never know when someone contacts you or sends you a message unless you check it.

TWITTER

Here is how Twitter describes itself: "Twitter is an American online news and social networking service on which users post and interact with messages known as 'tweets.' Tweets were originally restricted to 140 characters, but on November 7, 2017, this limit was doubled for all languages except Chinese, Japanese, and Korean."

There are 261 million international Twitter users, which account for 79 percent of Twitter accounts that are based outside the United States. There are more than 69 million Twitter users in the US. Roughly 46 percent of Twitter users are on the platform daily. The total number of Twitter users in the UK is 13 million.

The following are some tips about Twitter:

Tip 1: Mind the kind. You must always be kind and not say negative things about anyone or any company. The reason—your Tweet can be retweeted to hundreds or even thousands of other people. That means people can take your tweet and resend it. Also be careful not to say anything profane or inappropriate. Tweeting is public—meaning anyone, including your employer, can see it.

Tip 2: Follow others. On Twitter you can follow someone you like or admire. A good way to network and connect is to follow someone and watch when they post, then comment on it. The goal is to connect with people.

Tip 3: Picture this. Just like on LinkedIn, you should have your profile picture on Twitter so people know who they are connecting with—a real human being. When you create your Twitter name, known as a handle, it is something like @JSWilson. Our CEO's handle is @Motivator. Don't choose a goofy name or anything too cute like @pinkmonkey. Keep your handle professional.

LinkedIn and Twitter are two great ways to connect and communicate. You just have to use each wisely. Remember to be polite, kind, and professional *at all times.*

"You may have a small network, but growing that network has become easier with the

use of social tools. LinkedIn, Conspire, even Facebook and Twitter allow you to grab branches that may have previously seemed out of reach."

—DAVID COHEN

Networking

"Okay let's be honest, you're not networking for your health, and you are networking because you want to gain something, right? You want to increase sales, increase opportunities, grow your business, and build your network of connections or some other positive reason for networking. That is all true, but the key is when you are networking, either live or virtually, it is essential not to have the networking be about you."

–SHAWN DOYLE CSP

This chapter is about networking. If you think about it, networking is an interesting mix of communication and connection. You may not realize it but you are networking every day, except you may not be consciously aware of it. Networking comes in three forms:

1. Networking functions that are internal in your organization (cocktail receptions, a company meeting, company holiday party, trade shows, etc.)

2. Networking functions that are external (trade shows, association meetings, professional functions)

3. Networking virtually (LinkedIn, email (if used for that purpose), Facebook (sometimes used for business), Twitter

In this chapter, I cover only the first two. LinkedIn deserves its own chapter because there is so much to cover and it is such a rich resource for connection and communication.

INTERNAL NETWORKING FUNCTIONS

Let's face it, people get promoted based on three factors at work: 1) the ability to do work and get results; 2) your communication skills and ability to manage how people perceive you; 3) who you know. When discussions come up about promotions and executives are talking, their decisions are based on the quality of work and track record, but make no mistake they also are swayed by perception and how well they like someone. Also keep in mind you never know who is involved in making decisions about you, so everyone counts.

Most people have attended company meetings, conferences, trade shows, and training programs. These are all networking opportunities. As Sallie Krawcheck said, "Networking has been cited as the number one unwritten rule of success in business. *Who* you know really impacts *what* you know."

The following are some tips and techniques for networking:

Tip 1: Plan ahead. Do your people research. When you know you are going to be attending a networking event, do the research. Find out from the meeting planner who will be attending. Far too many times people stand at a cocktail reception and meet one of their senior executives and have *no idea* what to say. They are baffled and awkward and don't make a good impression. Let's change this scenario. What if when you meet the senior executive you say, "It's nice to meet you. We have something in common. I graduated from the same school as your daughter." They will light up and have a conversation with you—impressed that you know that. This information is easily available with an Internet search, looking them up on LinkedIn, or by reading their bio on your company website. This information is not hard to find.

Tip 2: When in Rome. For any networking event, check with the meeting planner and ask what the dress code is. If you know people who have attended previously, ask them as well. You want to dress at or above the dress code to make a favorable impression. If everyone is in a suit and tie you don't want to be the only one underdressed.

Tip 3: Them is us. The one *mindset* you want at any networking event is that it is all about the other people. It's not how they feel about you—it's how you make them feel about themselves. If you make them feel good about themselves, they will connect with you. The best way to do this and the best way to connect is to ask them questions about their personal and professional life. Ask open-ended questions that can only be answered with conversation, not a yes or no.

Here are some examples of the hundreds of questions you could ask:

- What is your role in the company?
- Have you always been in that role?
- How long have you been with your organization?
- What were you doing before you came here?
- What do you like most about it?
- How many people are on your team?
- How did your company find you when you started here?
- What challenges or changes in the industry are you seeing now?
- How is that different from what you saw in the past?

- How often do you travel in your role?
- What did you think of that news story about ____ last week? (industry related)
- What do you do when you're not working?
- Do you have a favorite sport or hobby?

Tip 4: Return volley. When you ask someone a question and receive an answer, it is important to respond positively and appropriately. Let's say you ask someone a question and they say, "I have been with the company for 24 years." Your response should be something like "Wow! Twenty-four years? That's amazing. Congratulations. By the way, I've noticed many people with long tenure here, which is impressive. In your opinion, why is that?" You will notice you are positively responding and asking another follow-up question, based on their response. When you give positive feedback, people want to talk more. It's a psychological reward.

Tip 5: Thumbs up. Always be positive. I think everyone wants to deal with people who are positive, upbeat, and energetic. At any network event you are part of, be positive. As John C. Maxwell said, "People may *hear* your words, but they *feel* your attitude." Be positive and don't say anything negative about people, companies, products, or circumstances. Let's say the company just laid off 500 people at an office in Milwaukee and someone asks you about it at a networking event. It would be best to say, "Yes I heard about that. I'm sure it will all work out in the long run." If there is a comment about someone such as, "I think our CEO Susan is a world-class jerk." Say something like, "Hmmm. I haven't had a chance to meet her yet." Say *nothing negative* and don't agree! Don't get involved and take the "gossip bait." Also keep in mind that you never know who knows who, or who is friends with someone at work. There are sometimes alliances you may not know about. Negative things always get back to people, and guess what—so do positive comments! "Hi, Imani. I was just at a networking event and Bill said some nice things about you!" Word travels. It will also reinforce your reputation as a positive person.

Tip 6: Drink not. This is a decision you have to make, but I think it is a bad idea to drink alcoholic beverages at company events. It leads to reduction of inhibitions, bad judgment, and doing things that can ruin your reputation. You have probably seen examples of that in your work life. Have a soda instead, no one will know you aren't drinking. As I often say, don't forget you are at a company event—and everyone is watching you. You need to keep your wits about you.

Tip 7: Information, please. When you start talking to people during networking, they will eventually, if they are good conversationalists, come around to asking you about yourself. You need to be prepared to know what you are going to say. Think of this as branding: How do you want to position yourself and what you do? What makes you unique and memorable? If you asked me at an event what I did I would say, "I'm Rachael and I'm the COO of Shawn Doyle training. We help professionals win at work." I would stop there. Then the other person would probably say, "Hmm…that's interesting. How do you do that?" So when you tell people what you do: 1) keep it short; and 2) make it compelling enough to make them ask a question. If you are in the marketing department, don't say, "I'm in marketing" that is yawn inducing. Say, "I make our products and services irresistible to our customers." See how that is so much better? Tell the story and tell it well. When people ask about sports or hobbies, again have a compelling answer. Don't say, "I love pro football." Say instead, "I'm a lifelong fan of the Green Bay Packers because I grew up there." That leads to more possible discussion. As Christine Lynch said, "Networking is marketing. Marketing yourself, your uniqueness, what you stand for."

Tip 8: Find it. The goal of networking is to connect and communicate. The best way to do that is to find something in common with the other person. It could be anything at all: 1) geography; 2) education; 3) hobbies; 4) knowing the same people; 5) the same industry in the past; 6) travel; 7) animals; 8) kids and family; 9) military; or 10) charity work.

If you are talking to someone and the person loves dogs and you love dogs…that's IT! You now have a connection and you start showing each other pictures of your dogs on your phones and exchanging dog stories. The person will also tell other people, "You'll never believe it! Amanda and I both have basset hounds!" Once you have made a connection, ask for a card if they have one—yes, even for people within your company.

Tip 9: Kick and goal! Make sure to have a goal. Why are you going to the networking except for the fact it is mandatory? What is the goal? Who do you want to connect with? Who do you want to meet? Why? Why would it be important to know them? Who could help your career? Make it a point to seek them out and say hello. You may be a little shy, maybe an introvert, but that will not serve you well. For networking you have to be bold and take risks. No matter where you work, politics matter more than you may know. Always be open to meeting new people—you may be pleasantly surprised!

Tip 10: Words have power. In the world we live in today, profanity has become more popular and we hear it a lot in comedy and in our society. Just because it is more common doesn't mean you should do it. Here is the key rule at work— no profanity ever. Why? If networking is about connection and communication, you will lose some percentage of your audience because they are offended by your language. They will shut down and you will fail in making a connection. Besides, in the era of so many cases of workplace harassment and sexual harassment, we need to be very cautious about our language. We don't want to be the example of harassing behavior.

Tip 11: Next. The question I always get is, "What do I do after a networking event?" The simple answer is do the *next step* in the process. That step is for you to decide. I suggest that after a networking event, as soon as possible write a list of all the people you have met. Then think about doing one of the following:

- Invite them to join you on LinkedIn.
- Send each a handwritten thank-you note.
- Call and touch base a week later.
- Send an email with a link to something they would like (video clip, article, a white paper, information, a website) and include a brief note such as, "I know we talked about our common interest in stamps, here is a cool article I found on rare stamps."
- Invite them to lunch, breakfast, or coffee if you are in the same geographical area.
- Refer them to a friend, coworker, or resource, saying, "I thought since we met and you indicated you were interested in block chain technology you might like to meet Juan who is an expert in block chain in my mind." If you can be a valuable resource, people will refer you to others.

Since networking is a process and not an event, take the next step, whatever that may be and make a connection.

Tip 12: Can I get a volunteer? Another great way to network is to volunteer for company committees. There are always planning committees, charity committees, safety committees, etc. in any organization. The great thing about being on a committee is it gives you exposure and you get to network with people you would not normally know or work with and a chance to network. It also positions you as someone who is willing to step up and take a leadership role, allowing you more time to interact with senior leadership.

Tip 13: Complimentary. When you network, give people authentic compliments. If you like the person's necklace, say so. If you like something they did at work, say so, "Hey, I really liked that marketing campaign." It is amazing how powerful a comment can be if it is sincere. People love positive feedback.

Tip 14: Ask the best question. I really love this technique and it works really well. The question at the end of meeting someone is this, "How can I help you?" Make sure if you ask this it's genuine and not just words. This often surprises people. I guess because no one asks, but they like the question. If they ask for clarification say, "Do you need resources, advice, sources, vendors, anything where you need more information." We recently asked one of our clients that question and he had a specific need, which was something we don't provide or do, so we referred him to a carefully vetted resource. Where did we find the resource? By asking people in our network, of course.

EXTERNAL NETWORKING FUNCTIONS

The reality is that almost all the same rules apply for external as for internal networking—except they may be even more important. Research, for example, becomes even more critical because you know nothing about their company.

Tip 1: Goal refined. Get a list of people who are going to attend and target 15-20 people you want to meet and network with and work on that as your goal. Prepare by researching those people. Don't spend all your time with one person; try to meet as many people as possible. This will maximize your networking effectiveness.

Tip 2: Don't be surprised. Every now and then when you network with people and contact them afterward, you never hear anything back. Oh well, that happens; some people don't understand the value of networking. There are more networking fish in the sea.

Tip 3: All hands on deck. When networking and meeting people, always smile, introduce yourself using your first and last name, ask their name, and shake their hand. Your handshake should be firm and confident and accompanied by eye contact. This is not the time to be shy.

As Bob Burg said, "Networking is simply the cultivating of mutually beneficial, give and take, win-win relationships. It works best, however, when emphasizing the 'give' part."

WHAT YOUR TABLE
SHOULD NOT LOOK
LIKE...

CHAPTER 8

Business Meal Guidelines, Part 1

"This idea of shared humanity and the connections that we make with one another— that's what, in fact, makes life worth living."
—CLINT SMITH

A big part of business is the business meal. It happens every day around the world. There are going to be many occasions where you will be invited to business meals—it may be a breakfast at the Chamber of Commerce, a lunch with a client, or a group dinner on a business trip. These are opportunities to connect, communicate, and bond with colleagues, coworkers, and anyone else you will work with, or want to work with, in a fun way. It can really make a big, positive difference in your professional relationships.

You can get to know someone on a different level and create great associations. That is the positive side of the equation. As reported in *Inc.* magazine, when Impraise, a performance-management software company based in New York, had just five employees, they all sat down and had lunch together; now, the company has more than 30 employees, and they still eat together at one large table. "We've found this has a great effect on maintaining open communication as we grow, ensuring that people never feel divided, even if we're working on different things," said Bas Kohnke, CEO of Impraise.

The bad news is, during business meals you can also make negative impressions. I have seen people make many social faux pas and blunders at business meals. The simple truth is that they can simply be avoided, with only a little education and awareness.

The following is some interesting information about business meals:

- Dinova, Inc. and The BTN Group partnered on a joint industry research study. According to the survey, 49 percent of respondents reported that his or her company spent

$1 million or more on business meals and entertainment expenses in 2016.

- A staggering number of people hit the roads and fly the friendly skies for business purposes each year. The Global Business Travel Association pegs the number of business trips taken annually in the United States at 488 million.

- The price of eating out while away from home sure adds up. Business Travel News puts the average daily spending for meals at $96.89.

Here are some valuable tips regarding business meals:

Tip 1: Watch it. One key cardinal rule for business meals is to arrive early, as arriving late is really bad form. Get there early, but not too early. If you arrive fifteen minutes early, wait in your car or freshen your makeup or comb your hair in the restroom. Use the time to refresh yourself about etiquette by looking at an etiquette app on your phone. Then arrive about five minutes early to the location. Being late implies you don't care about the other person's time. If a group meal, make sure to get the cell phone number of the host or of the person you're dining with if you're just dining with one person. If for some reason you have an emergency or you're caught up in an unexpected traffic jam (you should plan for this, but it can happen) and are going to be late, call the host or the person to inform them of the delay. When you arrive, apologize for being late and then move on. If you arrive before your host or another person you are going to dine with, let the host or hostess know you're expecting another guest and wait for them instead of sitting at the table. It can get confusing if they are waiting for you in the front and you are seated at the back.

Tip 2: Hello. If you are involved in a group dinner, when you arrive, make eye contact with and shake hands with each person and introduce yourself. Say something positive like, "It's nice to meet you," or if you know them, say, "It's good to see you again." The host may not be able to make introductions, so it is up to you to take initiative and introduce yourself. Smile and try to remember each person's name. One way to remember a name is to repeat it out loud, "It's nice to meet you, Jay." Don't just introduce yourself to one person and not everyone else. Mingle and say hello to everyone.

Tip 3: Take a seat. Generally speaking, if you are part of a group dinner, a smart host (usually the one who invited everyone to the dinner) will suggest a place for you to sit. If not, do not sit at either end of the table, those are chairs for people who have the most power or for the person who is hosting the meal.

Tip 4: Wait a minute. When having a meal with anyone, be courteous and kind to the server, and ask for the server's name if not on the name tag. I have witnessed many times when a business meal diner was extremely rude to the server, which made a negative impression on the other person(s) present for the meal. You can demonstrate your professionalism by treating everyone with courtesy and respect. It is *never acceptable to be rude.* I was once interviewing a candidate for a position in a company; he told me how he loved people and he was a very empathetic person. When the server came to the table to check and see if everything was okay, he snapped at the server and was extremely rude. Needless to say he did not get the job offer. Whoops.

Tip 5: Don't lead, follow. If you are having a business meal and the person orders first, try to follow that lead. For example, if you are having lunch in an Italian restaurant and the person orders a sandwich, don't order a giant platter of spaghetti. There's actually a practical reason for this—the other person will be finished eating way before you and will have to wait until you are done. The same approach applies to dessert. If you are involved in a group dinner and the server comes around with the dessert menu and everyone else declines dessert, don't be the one person who orders dessert. Why? Because the rules of etiquette say that if someone orders dessert, then everyone has to *wait* until that person has finished their dessert until anyone can leave. The same applies for alcoholic beverages. If no one else is ordering an alcoholic beverage, you should not either. I know you may say, "But I want dessert!" Well, I understand, but business meals are not about what you want, they are about making connections, building relationships, and communication. Be aware of what is going on around you.

Tip 6: Ask. If you are dining with someone who has been at that particular restaurant before, it is a good idea to ask for recommendations. First, it shows that you value their opinion and second, it appeals to their ego if you are asking for their recommendation for a food choice. It's another way to make a connection.

Tip 7: The phone zone. If you are having a business meal, you should be very careful about using the phone. I believe the phone should *not* be used during the meal *at all*. When you arrive at the restaurant, silence your phone— and under no circumstances should you look at your phone, text message, or answer any emails while you are dining. Of course, there are notable exceptions. If you have an emergency, then politely explain, "Just so you know, I'm expecting an urgent call. I don't think they're going to call during our meal, but if they do, I may have to take the call." Most people don't mind this if they have been forewarned in advance. If those kinds of calls come and you have to answer the phone, answer the phone, gesture to the other person that you will be right back, and step away to a private area to take the call. This is rare and should be the exception, not the rule. As a guideline, there should be nothing placed on the table—not your phone, keys, eyeglasses or case, purse, wallet, gloves, or hats. Nothing should be on the table except plates and food.

Tip 8: May I have your full attention. When dining with someone, give them your full and undivided attention. As mentioned in the last tip, do not look at your phone, but also do not give in to the temptation to look around the room, which may be distracting. I have noticed that many restaurants now have added lots of televisions to their environment that are often broadcasting any manner of major league sports programming. These huge TV screens can be enormously distracting as they are showing sports action. You don't want to be the person who is having a conversation while looking over the person's shoulder at the screen behind them. Maintain eye contact and attention to help the person feel valued and connected with.

Tip 9:   It's not a motivational seminar but... Stay positive. One great way to connect with other people at business meals is to always stay positive. People want to be around and talk to people who are positive, upbeat, and optimistic. You want people to feel good after talking with you. The general guideline is to never say anything negative about anyone, or as the famous quote my parents used to say to me, "If you can't say anything nice, don't say anything at all." If someone tries to draw you into a negative conversation during a meal, try to change the topic to something more positive. As Wade Boggs said, "A positive attitude causes a chain reaction of positive thoughts, events, and outcomes. It is a catalyst and it sparks extraordinary results."

Tip 10: No Maybelline. Here is a good guideline. No makeup application at the table. If you are having a business meal with one person or a group, you should never *under any circumstances* apply makeup at the table. If you need to touch up lipstick or check your makeup, simply excuse yourself and go to the restroom. The same applies to men if wondering if you have a piece of lettuce stuck in your teeth or if you're having a bad hair day—excuse yourself and go to the restroom.

Tip 11: Battle of the tab. There are going to be times at a business meal when deciding who picks up the tab. Generally speaking, it is acknowledged that the host of the meal is supposed to pick up the tab, regardless of gender. If you are taking a customer for a business meal, it is a given that you should pick up the tab. If two people go out for a business meal and each one is the equal and work for the same company, you can decide how to handle the tab when it arrives, or just split it. One elegant way of making sure there is no issue is to arrive early, find your server, and give your server your credit card *before* the meal so there's no issue about who's going to pay the tab. Anytime someone else picks up the tab for a business meal, always thank them. If they pay, it's good form to offer to pay the tip. If there is no host or several people are going to split the tab, bring enough cash to make it easy.

Tip 12: I'll have a little. Appetizers are tricky when it comes to a business meal, obviously there's not going to be that issue with breakfast, but it can come up at lunch and dinner. The best approach to appetizers is to follow the lead of the other person you're dining with. If the person orders an appetizer first, you can order. If not, you shouldn't. This is for a very simple and practical reason as stated previously, if you order an appetizer it will take longer and the other person has to wait. If you're dining with a group and the server asks about appetizers, make sure you know who the host of the meal is, as he or she will be the one to give guidance to the server about appetizers and about alcoholic beverages. In many cases, I have seen the host of the dinner order a variety of appetizers for the entire table and everyone shares. If asked for suggestions, you can suggest one.

Tip 13: Try everything. Unless you are allergic to something that's being served or have some other nutritional restriction, it is considered polite to try everything, at least a little. For example, if the host orders a range of appetizers and raves about a particular dish, it is polite to at least try a little of it to show respect for the host. Don't ever say you don't like something or criticize the food. You may unknowingly criticize something they chose.

Tip 14: Say please and thank you. Any time you are having a business meal, you should always say, "Please" and "Thank you" to the host, to your servers, and to the folks involved in providing your meal, such as people who provide water or bread. I know it sounds somewhat simplistic, but if you say please and thank you to everyone and show sincere appreciation, you show everyone around you that you are the kind of person other people want to do business with.

Tip 15: Avoid the verboten. There are three topics to avoid during a business meal—politics, sex, religion. Each is explained in more detail, in no particular order:

1. Politics. No matter how hard you try, no matter who you're with, the topic of politics is going to become controversial and you stand a chance of offending at least 50 percent of the people with whom you're dining. No one wants to have a meal that includes a heated political argument. In the world of business, you should try as much as possible to be apolitical, neutral. If someone tries to bait you into a political conversation, just smile and artfully change the topic. As a training and development company, we do many live training programs across the country every year. Many times during live training programs, participants bring up a political issue. Our facilitators, being trained professionals, can politely redirect the conversation away from politics back to the business topic at hand. You would be surprised at how often it happens.

2. Sex. Another topic you want to avoid during business meals is the topic of sex or sexual innuendos. I know these days it is often a popular topic in the news, but it doesn't mean it should be coming up at the dinner table. Also realize in today's litigious world that if you are a leader or in any position of authority in a company, conversation of a sexual nature during a meal could lead to a problem with liability for harassment. Use common sense and simply avoid those topics.

3. Religion. This is a zero-sum game—avoid speaking about religion at all costs. You can't win and will often lose on the topic of religion. As Brett and Kate McKay said, "When it comes to avoiding the topics of politics, religion, and money with new acquaintances—folks you've just met—there's a reason this piece of advice is so timeworn. The introduction of these 'controversial' subjects can lead to a conversation getting overly heated, create misunderstandings, cause people to take offense, and end a relationship before it's even begun." Not a great way to connect.

Tip 16: Wow! Compliment the restaurant's food and the place. In many cases the people who arranged the business meal are proud of the selection they made and are excited to share with you a great restaurant in terms of its food, ambience, or location. Make sure to compliment the person who chose the venue and the location because this validates the choices and the person will feel appreciated for the choices. You can say something like, "What a great menu," or "What a beautiful view," or "This lobster bisque is fantastic." Thanking the person for the selection is both professional and gracious and yet another way to bond and connect.

Last, always end the meal by thanking the host and the person who joined you. Send a follow-up thank-you email, or better yet, a handwritten thank-you note, which is always a big winner.

> *"My idea of a good night has always been having a lovely meal and a proper conversation."*
> —KIRSTY GALLACHER

WHAT MANY PEOPLE WISH THEY HAD AT DINNER...

CHAPTER 9

Business Meal Guidelines, Part 2

"Good manners will open doors that the best education cannot."
—CLARENCE THOMAS

Every time you have a business meal you have a chance to make an impression—good or not so good. It may be a meal with a coworker, with a boss or executive in your organization, or with clients and vendors. Either way, it is an opportunity to shape how people perceive you, get to know people better, and to connect.

The following are some additional important tips to be aware of when it comes to business meals:

Tip 1: **Follow the host.** A great guideline when dining for business is to follow what the host is doing. If you're having lunch and the host orders a salad, you may want to follow suit. If you are at dinner and the host orders an alcoholic beverage, feel free to do so. If the host does not order an alcoholic beverage, it's best to skip it.

Tip 2: **The fork in the road.** When seated at a business dinner, remember that your water glass is to your right and your bread plate is always on your left. Remembering this will prevent you from accidentally drinking from someone else's water glass or accidentally stealing their bread. A formal place setting at the table is a guide to your meal. The amount of silverware tells you how many courses will be served. A general guideline is to start on the outside and work your way in toward your plate. On the left side is your salad fork and your dinner fork. On the right side is a spoon, your salad knife, and dinner knife. Any fork or spoon placed at the top of your plate is your dessert spoon and fork. On your left you will see a bread plate that includes a small butter spreader style knife; use it only for your bread.

See that wasn't so hard, was it? Once you know the layout, that is. Be careful to use your own utensils and not the person's next to you. As Dennis Cornell, an expert on business protocol, said, "For many families there is no regular dining time anymore, so many young people don't learn what the rules are. This puts them at a significant disadvantage in a move out into the real world because the mastery of etiquette is supposed to reveal important parts of one's character and competence."

Tip 3: Sit tight. When you arrive at your table, notice if there are any place cards with names for seating. This is often done at business and social events. If there are none, wait until others arrive before being seated. The accepted way of sitting down is from the right side, and if you are getting out the chair, from the right side. If you have to get up from the table for some reason, excuse yourself and quietly leave the table. You don't have to explain why you are leaving to anyone. See the next tip for what to do with your napkin when you leave.

Tip 4: Where is the napkin? If you're eating in a restaurant where the utensils are wrapped up in the napkin, simply unwrap your utensils and place your napkin in your lap. Despite scenes you may have seen in movies, you should never, ever, ever tuck your napkin into the front of your shirt. That should stay in the movies. The key rule for your napkin is if you have to leave the table, it actually should be placed on your empty chair to indicate to the server that you plan to return. Keep in mind that some of these practices will make a positive impression, but some are also designed as a *courtesy to your servers* so they don't have to guess.

Tip 5:   The big spender. Don't be the big spender. If you are at a group meal and you are ordering from the menu, do not order the most expensive item. Order something in the middle range. If someone is buying your meal, it is considered rude to order the most expensive item on the menu. The only exception is if the host is strongly encouraging people to order a certain dish that is the specialty of the house and it happens to be the most expensive item. Then order that if you want to.

Tip 6:   The starting line. Don't eat until *everyone* has been served. If you are part of a group meal, it is considered good manners to wait until everyone has been served before eating. I have seen on many occasions when the server brings the first four or five dishes and yet they're still ten more people waiting for their food, those already served start eating. Rather, you should politely wait until everyone has been served to begin eating.

Tip 7:   Hold up. If you are not aware of it, there are basically two ways to hold your utensils at a business meal, or at any meal really. You can hold your utensils either *continental style* which is sometimes called European-style, or *American-style*. There is no one style that is right, just familiarize yourself with one style and use one consistently. If you don't know the correct way to hold your utensils, you can certainly look up videos on YouTube, or articles on the Internet to tell you and show you the two different styles. The following website may be helpful: https://workology.com/manner-monday-american-vs-continental-style-dining/.

Tip 8: Take the cut. The general guideline for eating your entrée is to cut one bite at a time. Because you're not feeding it to a five-year-old, you do not need to cut all your food into small pieces before eating any. This also applies to salads, you should cut salad up one bite at a time.

Tip 9: Call me. If you are attending a business meal, under no circumstances should you look at your phone or answer a call, unless it is an absolute emergency. Your phone should not even be out or on the table. If for some reason you have to answer a call, simply excuse yourself from the table, go somewhere private, and take the call or call the person back. Your phone should definitely be on silent or vibrate, because the last thing you want during the meal is for your phone to break out in some sort of song. This will immediately get you attention, but the wrong kind. The latest top tune loudly blaring from somewhere on your person does not necessarily make a great impression. I have noticed recently that Amtrak has started having quiet cars on all of their trains. Clearly, I believe, one of the reasons is because people are so rude when using their phones—talking loudly, having loud, blaring phone ringtones, and not being aware of or having respect for other people around them. People go to the quiet cars for some peace.

Tip 10: There is a season. I don't know if this is true, but I have heard many famous stories of people who have failed during job interviews because they salted their food before they tasted it. I don't know if this is true or urban myth, however, why take chances? If you are having a business meal, taste your food before putting any seasoning on the food whether salt or pepper. The assumption is that people think you are making a judgment about your food before tasting it.

Tip 11: On the table. For some reason it has become very popular for people to carry around multiple devices such as cell phones and iPads. Some people even have one cell phone for work and one for home. I often see people when dining place both cell phones and keys and sunglasses on the table. The general guideline is to place nothing on the table; whatever you bring along should stay below the table, either in your briefcase or in your purse, but not on the table—it takes up room and is considered rude.

Tip 12: To-go, no. As tempting as it is, if you're attending a business meal and there are leftovers, you should *never ask* for a to-go box. In your personal life that is fine, but it is considered bad form at a business meal to ask to take your food with you.

Tip 13: Keep it to yourself. If you're having a business meal and the food or the service is bad, *don't say anything negative*. Other people may make comments, but do not complain or criticize. This is important for two reasons: 1) you don't want to look like a complaining, negative person— who wants to work with someone like that? and 2) if the host selected the restaurant, you're actually insulting the host's choice. As my mom always said, "If you can't say something nice, don't say anything at all."

Tip 14: Pointer, please. As a general guideline, never use any of your utensils as a pointer during conversations. Picking up your steak knife and jabbing it in the air to make a point about something that you're passionate about looks slightly threatening and is considered rude. Just like you would not point a finger at someone, you should not point a utensil at someone.

Tip 15: Wine, please. There may be occasions where the host will be very polite and ask you to order the wine. If you are not a wine expert and you don't feel comfortable ordering, ask the host for suggestions or ask the waiter or the wine steward for advice. After the bottle of wine is opened, it is customary for the server to bring a glass of wine to the person who made the selection to taste it and give approval. If you're the person who did the selecting, this would be you. Take a small sip, smile and say, "This is wonderful," or something else positive.

Tip 16: Stay that again. The unbreakable rule about business dining is you must stay until everyone is finished eating. If there is a group of eighteen people and the server asks if anyone would like dessert, if one person orders dessert, then everyone has to stay until that person has been served and has finished his or her meal. There are no exceptions to this rule; it is considered extremely rude to leave early. This also works in reverse, if you're thinking about ordering dessert or an after-dinner cocktail, notice if other people are too. If no one else is ordering, politely decline. You don't want to be the reason everyone has to stay longer than necessary.

Tip 17: The pair. If someone asks you to pass the salt, it is considered good manners to pass both the salt and pepper at the same time. Doing this indicates that you're very familiar with business etiquette, and also prevents the person from having to also ask for the pepper.

Tip 18: Drop it. If for some reason during the meal you drop a utensil, you should never pick it up from the floor. Just leave it there and quietly ask your server for a replacement. The same rules apply if you drop your napkin just ask your server for another napkin.

> "Manners are a sensitive awareness of the feelings of others. If you have that awareness, you have good manners, no matter what fork you use."
> —EMILY POST

ENDANGERED SPECIES...

HANDWRITTEN THANK-YOU NOTE

CHAPTER 10

Holidays, Birthdays, and Other Celebrations

"Company parties are fun, but you should never forget where you are. Go right ahead and enjoy the celebration with your coworkers while you maintain your professionalism while you remember that you'll have to face these people on Monday."
—DEBBY MAYNE

One of our clients (not mentioning any names, of course) was telling us a story about attending a company holiday party.

At the party, a senior executive approached the client to say hello and he very quickly realized that the executive could barely stand up because he was extremely intoxicated. As our client stated so candidly, "I could never look at him the same way again."

If you work in a corporate environment, a government agency, or a nonprofit, there will always be workplace celebrations—birthday, baby shower, promotion, work anniversary, or any number of holidays. Being able to navigate the landscape of celebrations is critically important because it is a chance for you to connect and communicate with others. That being said, it also takes some discretion and artfulness as celebrating at work can be interesting *and* it can affect your career.

The following are some tips about celebrations at work:

Tip 1:   Good times. Make it fun. Since we're talking about having celebrations and celebrating some sort of special occasion, it's important to make sure that it's fun. One part of fun is to make sure that any celebration event is voluntary and people are not required to attend. When celebrations become mandatory, that's when people start begrudging the celebration and not having as much fun as they could. In my opinion, all event celebrations should be voluntary.

Tip 2:   Small is big. If you are having a birthday celebration or a baby shower for a team member, it is probably a good idea to keep it small, meaning restricted to your department. Larger celebrations, like the holiday party, may involve the entire organization; but generally speaking, keeping a celebration small is a good idea. Smaller celebrations are easier to manage, require less space, and are not as involved.

Tip 3: No coercion. At one point at work you probably experienced someone approaching you and saying, "We're having a party for Lola. I'm sure you would like to make a contribution for a gift for her...*wouldn't you?*" Unfortunately, the person asking made people feel uncomfortable if they don't want to contribute, or made it feel like it was an obligation. Another idea is to send an envelope around, that way people who want to can contribute and those who don't want to don't feel pressured.

Tip 4: What a fascinating world. We now live in a very diverse world and that diversity includes people of different religious and cultural persuasions. When having celebrations, we have to be extremely careful to not have people feel like they are required to attend and/or participate. Yes, there are people who do not celebrate certain holidays and do not want to participate. When someone states they're not interested in participating in holiday celebrations, be respectful and don't force them to participate.

Tip 5: Hi, everyone. Everyone knows about office politics. When it comes to an office celebration, that is not the time to include office politics. The best and most graceful way to handle any office celebration is to invite everyone and let them decide if they want to attend or not. For example, let's say Fred is retiring in your department and there is a small group of people planning for Fred's retirement party. Generally speaking, everyone in the department should be invited so that no one feels left out or slighted. The idea behind a celebration is to have people feel good about it and not to hurt feelings.

Tip 6:   Thank you, shouldn't have. If you have a celebration like a holiday party and you decide that people should exchange or bring gifts, make sure that the suggested amount for the gift is a modest one. The idea behind a gift exchange is not for people to resent having to invest a great deal of money, but to have fun exchanging gifts.

Tip 7:   Invitation, please. In the modern world, many people have gotten away from sending paper invitations for celebrations in the office. I personally believe that paper invitations are more elegant and are perceived more positively and even create a more positive perception of the celebration. I understand that everyone has busy schedules and the convenience of email, so if you choose to send electronic invitations—and there are many services who do this—then ask people to electronically RSVP. I think it is okay in an office environment to send electronic invitations. One general guideline that I strongly recommend is that you give people enough notice about an upcoming celebration. With people being extremely busy at work as well as at home, advanced planning and giving people ample notice is an act of courtesy.

Tip 8:   It's still business. No matter what form of celebration is happening, please always remember that you are still at work, and you are not out with your friends or family. Please keep in mind that when you're attending a company social event, you will be observed by people who can make important decisions about your career. You do not want them to have a negative perception of you. For example, let's say at the company event there is a karaoke DJ, and everyone is singing their favorite songs. That is fine. But if you are the one person who sings your song wearing a moose hat, jumping from table to table, and tearing off your shirt at the end of your amazing performance, it may be damaging to your career. Just remember to be on your best behavior. You can do the crazy stuff, if you like, with your friends and family, but don't post it on Facebook—employers look at that too. According to business etiquette expert Hilka Klinkenberg, "The cardinal rule is to remember that no matter how festive the occasion, it's still about business. Don't fall off the fast track to success or risk damaging your professional reputation in one night of inadvertent blunders."

Tip 9: Watch yourself. A few months ago, my husband and I were having dinner at a nice restaurant. While we were waiting for our table, we noticed a family with a mom and dad and two children. The family ended up being seated near our table and we were able to figure out that they were celebrating one of the children's birthdays. With the rest of the dinner before them, they were obsessed with taking pictures of their appetizers, their dinner, and their desserts and posting them to various social media. This was a personal event, so it was fine. However, when you are at company celebration events, be extremely careful about taking pictures and posting them to social media—particularly if you're posting pictures of people who are acting a little too silly or in an unprofessional manner. First, this can be very embarrassing for the person who sees the picture on Facebook the next day, or could potentially be embarrassing for the company in the image that is presented to the public at large. Second, be very careful about letting other people take your picture when you're dancing at the holiday party wearing giant sunglasses. Just remember the Internet is forever! As Julie Blais Comeau said, "Before you put photos on Facebook, consider this: Whatever you want to post, imagine putting it on your fridge at home and see if the pictures are appropriate if your kids walk by. The second fridge is at work. If your coworkers or boss walks by, is it still okay?"

Tip 10: Red, red wine. If you look back and read Tip 8 again, the entire tip is about not acting in a way that is inappropriate. One way to ensure that you will act *inappropriately* is having too much alcohol at a company celebration. Yes we know, we have had people tell us that they had a company culture that believes in working hard and playing hard, which I understand. But we have to be very careful because this can lead to a very a bad perception of yourself. If you get intoxicated, it's possible that you can create a tremendous company liability. This is why many companies have started to steer away from offering alcohol at company events at all. If you wish to drink at a company celebration, drink in moderation; but my advice is to not drink at all, save your wine for family and personal time. This way you end up looking like the one who is professional and levelheaded all the time.

Tip 11: Be positive. One great guideline to follow when at a company celebration is to be positive. No one wants to have a conversation with someone who is extremely negative or pessimistic. Be upbeat, be positive, be energetic, and above all be kind. You can never go wrong with being positive, but you can go wrong by being negative.

Tip 12: Thanks. When you arrive at a company celebration event, seek out the people who planned the event and the people who were the sponsors and thank them for inviting you. When the event is over, try to again seek out your host and your planners and thank them for inviting you and tell them that you're going to be leaving. After the event, it is a good idea to send a handwritten thank-you note letting them know you had a good time and you sincerely appreciated being invited. If a handwritten note is just not possible to fit into your schedule, then an email thank-you is a must. Thanking people demonstrates that you are courteous, well mannered, and a professional.

Tip 13: Not work. When at an office celebration, try to limit your conversation to social conversation, not work conversation. Most people go to an office celebration to have a good time and relax, not to talk about the latest project or issues and problems in the company. Try to keep the conversation light and social.

Tip 14: The magic three. I'm sure you've heard this a million times, but there are three subjects you should never bring up in a social situation, because each are potential landmines. At company celebration events, you should never bring up: 1) sex; 2) politics; or 3) religion. We could almost add a fourth category—anything controversial. Avoid these topics because they are inappropriate and discussions often lead to people becoming emotionally involved and getting upset. No matter what, these topics will have at least half of your group disagreeing with what you're saying or wanting to insert their passionate opinion. The last thing you want at a company celebration is an argument or dispute. If people do bring up one of these subjects, switch to a more appropriate topic. This signals that you're not interested in talking about politics, sex, or religion. One other note, in this era of profuse sexual harassment litigation, the topic of sex in a conversation is extremely risky. Just don't go there.

Tip 15: Networking opportunity knocks. Another way to think of a holiday celebration is that it may be an opportunity to network and meet other people you've not had a lot of exposure to in the company. This may be an excellent opportunity to meet some of your key executives you never had much of a chance to talk to. What you may want to do is research some of the key executives by looking at their LinkedIn profiles, Google information, or company website biographies, and find a piece of information that you can talk to them about that they may find interesting. If you meet a key executive, you may say to her, "I understand that golf is a passion of yours." When she answers in the affirmative, you can then say something related to your golf experiences or lack of golf experience. This will probably lead to some interesting discussion. Although it may seem as if you are being spontaneous, you actually prepared talking points for when speaking with that executive socially. Although it may seem a bit contrived, being prepared is what socially successful people do.

Tip 16: Hands up. If you are attending a company celebration and you are holding a beverage, make sure to hold the beverage in your nondominant hand, the hand you do not shake with. This way when you meet someone, you'll to be able to shake the person's hand without juggling your drink or offering them a cold, wet hand as it has been holding your perspiring drink glass prior to shaking hands.

Tip 17: Eat first. When I say eat first, I mean have a snack or some food before you attend the company celebration. The purpose or the goal of these celebrations is to talk to other people, not to get a giant plate of food and sit down for an entire meal. If you eat beforehand, you can either skip food or eat lightly. This gives you a chance to talk and connect with more people.

"A nice note of thanks to the person responsible for organizing that lavish, super-fantastic office party is a sure way to be recognized and stand out in the New Year."
—LISA GACHÉ

Handling Social Situations at Work

"Practice self-awareness, self-evaluation, and self-improvement. If we are aware that our manners—language, behavior, and actions— are measured against our values and principles, we are able to more easily embody the philosophy; leadership is a matter of how to be, not how to do."

—FRANCES HESSELLEBEIN

Every day we go to work, we are faced with certain social situations, and some of them can be a challenge. If your goal is to connect and communicate with people in your office, then you need to practice self-awareness, self-evaluation, and know how you impact those around you. One person doesn't change an organization, but a collection of good people can!

As Kate Reardon said, "It doesn't matter how many A levels you have, what kind of degree you have, if you have good manners people will like you."

According to a recent survey from the staffing firm Accountemps, more than eight in ten (85 percent) of survey respondents say being courteous to coworkers has an impact on a person's *career prospects.*

In a study by the Center for Professional Excellence at York College in Pennsylvania. The Polk-Lepson Research Group surveyed 629 human resource and management professionals for their "Professionalism in the Workplace" study. Those who took the survey cite that the four indicators of professionalism are:

1. Interpersonal skills (33.6 percent)
2. Work ethic (27.3 percent)
3. Appearance (25.3 percent)
4. Communication skills (24.9 percent)

One-third of the human resource and management professionals surveyed state that they believe *professionalism has declined over the past three years.* Nearly two-thirds of those surveyed disagree with the idea that the perceived lack of professionalism is due to generational differences. The executive and management professionals stated that the best way to increase professionalism for new employees is to increase education. Once the new hires have onboarded, 30 percent of those surveyed believe there should be more business etiquette workshops.

It is important to know how to handle these social situations at work in an artful manner for people to have a positive perception of you.

The following are people and social situations that you often experience at work:

Tip 1: Are you coming? In our work situations, it is inevitable that associates may invite you to a personal event. It may be a wedding or wedding shower, a child's graduation, or someone's birthday party or retirement party. If someone invites you to a social event and you want to go, you can enthusiastically accept the invitation. The delicate part is if you do not wish to or cannot attend, then it is best to politely decline. Please note if you get an invitation electronically or on paper, always RSVP to the invite.

Tip 2: Are you happy? As a training company, one of the most frequent questions our facilitators are asked during training is about "happy hours" and whether people are required or obligated to attend. Let's say it's a Friday afternoon and everybody on the team is going out to happy hour and you receive either an email or a verbal invite. If you don't want to go, simply say "Thank you for inviting me, but unfortunately I can't make it. I have a conflict," or, "I have other plans." Always be gracious and thank the person who invited you. The challenge in the workplace is if you never go along to happy hour, people may start to develop a negative perception about you. You may want to occasionally go to happy hour. Go for 30 minutes, have a soda, and then leave. Showing up says you're willing to be a team player.

Tip 3: The boss. There may be occasions when someone who is a coworker and close friend gets promoted and becomes your boss. First, no matter how you feel about it, be gracious and congratulate the person for their promotion. Second, you must realize that while your after-hours, personal relationship as friends may stay the same, your work relationship should be professional and you should always respect the position as your manger or supervisor.

Tip 4: Boss-imposed, forced socializing. My husband used to have a boss years ago who, on a quarterly basis, invited everyone on his team to go out for half a day on his boat—on a Saturday. Although on the surface this sounds like a nice experience, it was well known that you *did not* decline the boss's invitation because it would be bad for your career. Additionally, this voluntary-mandatory event was also taking up precious time on the weekend. If this happens to you, you have to decide how important it is to your career. It may be necessary to decline on occasion; however, think about how important it is to your career and in your company culture. While I personally believe all that should matter is your work performance, I have learned from my experience in the corporate world that your social presence or lack of it can affect your perception as a "team player."

Tip 5: Fired up. No matter where you work, there are going to be occasions when, sadly, someone gets terminated from the company. What do you say, how do you talk about? The answer is you *say nothing* and you don't talk about it, because no good can come from that discussion. If someone says, "Wow, did you hear that Paul got fired yesterday afternoon?" Simply say, "Yes I heard." If that person tries to engage in further conversation about the poor soul who should have or maybe should not have been fired, just simply decline to discuss it by saying politely, "I really would rather not talk about it," and smile.

Tip 6: Happy happy. They're going to be occasions when a coworker has a birthday that everyone wants to celebrate. If you want to have a small get-together with your team to celebrate the birthday, there is certainly nothing wrong with that. If you want to give them a card signed by everyone on the team, that is a nice touch, or if you want to get a cake that is also very kind. The key to celebrations, is to make them voluntary, with no pressure on anyone who wants to decline.

Tip 7: Sad day. Unfortunately, someone you work with will lose a loved one. This is when tremendous empathy and sensitivity is required. First, sending a sympathy card to the person's home, whether from the department or individually, is always appropriate and most kind. If you and your family would like to send flowers, that is a nice touch. You can even send flowers from your departmental team. Read the obituary and see what the family has designated; sometimes families prefer a donation in lieu of flowers. When you have information about the service, if you can go, it means a great deal to attend and support your coworker. I have often heard from others how much it means to them when someone is kind enough to attend their loved one's services and pay their respects. Sheryl Sandberg, COO of Facebook, wrote a book about grief, and she writes that when she came back to work after her husband passed away, she wished people would have spoken to her. Instead of speaking to her, every time they saw her walk by, they just looked away because they didn't want to upset her. Many times people don't know what to say to someone who is grieving. I believe the best approach is to say you're sorry for their loss, and let them know you'd be happy to help them in any way you can. No more needs to be said, unless they want to discuss their loved one with you. Just listen and show that you care. If you would like to learn more, the CEO of our company, Shawn Doyle, wrote a book about grief titled *The Sun Still Rises: Surviving and Thriving after Grief and Loss.* It has helpful tips and information about handling grief.

Tip 8: Don't say it. For some reason, many people in the workplace like to talk about others in a negative way—the all too familiar gossip or rumor mill. My strong advice is not to participate in either of those practices. If someone attempts to gossip with you about another employee, just simply rebuff them by saying, "My mom always taught me if I can't say anything nice then to say nothing at all," and smile. Of course, you have to come up with the line that you're comfortable with, but gossip and spreading rumors will only hurt your career and hurt other people's feelings. Take the high ground and don't gossip about anyone, ever.

Tip 9: Cup courtesy. One great technique for connecting with and being courteous to others is if you are going to the break area to get a cup of coffee, ask coworkers around you if they would like a cup of coffee as well. If you're going down the street to buy some coffee at everyone's favorite coffee place, let people know you're going and ask if they would like you to pick up something. This shows courtesy and caring. It creates a nice work area and kindness spreads—it really does!

Tip 10: Kids play. In every workplace, people will always ask if you would like to contribute to their child's fundraiser, whether raising money for their school, Girl Scouts, Boy Scouts, or any other range of charities. Also on occasion, people participate in charity runs or other charitable events and will ask you to contribute in order to raise money for charity. If someone asks you to contribute, do it gladly. If you do not wish to, you can simply smile and say, "Thank you for asking but I already made a contribution to the charity of my choice." If you happen to be the person doing the asking, like asking others to buy candy bars to support your child's fundraising drive, ask in a light, friendly way with no pressure; and if someone says no, thank the person and leave it at that.

Tip 11: Uh oh, social media. Many of our clients tell us that in their organization there have been occasions when people have embarrassed themselves on social media, whether Facebook, Twitter, or Instagram. They may have written or posted some embarrassing content under their name or went on one of those social media channels and wrote something negative or inappropriate about the company. This can get someone terminated quickly. The best way to handle this is the same way you handle gossip if it comes up—decline to comment on it. Some companies have now added social media company policies.

Tip 12: Greetings. It is generally thought of as good manners to say hello when arriving at work and goodbye when leaving your department at the end of the day. It is a good idea to say goodnight to people in your work area to let them know that you're departing. If you see someone in the hallway, on the elevator, in the lobby, or in your parking lot, wave and say hello or goodbye depending on the time of day. I have seen cases where people walk by a coworker and say hello and a coworker says nothing in return. This makes a very negative impression and is rude. A simple nod or a hello is important to acknowledge your coworkers.

Tip 13: Elevate. It seems as if there is some sort of strange rule in the universe that people are not allowed to communicate on elevators. As LZ Granderson said, "Complete strangers can stand silent next to each other in an elevator and not even look each other in the eye. But at a concert, those same strangers could find themselves dancing and singing together like best friends." If you get on an elevator and a coworker is on the elevator with you, always give them a polite greeting. This is just a simple social courtesy.

Tip 14: Sick call. If you are sick, and I mean really, really sick—sneezing, coughing or wheezing—you're much better off to stay home and not share your virus with everyone on the team at work. I know that the inherent problem is bosses and companies put pressure on people not to call in sick and you don't want to be seen as the slacker. But the reality is, it is bad manners to go to work and share your germs with your coworkers. Use common courtesy. If you must sneeze or cough, grab a tissue. Or, turn your head and cough into your left upper sleeve, not your bare hands. This is not just my suggestion but the advice of the CDC and the American Public Health Association.

Tip 15: The helper. In your workplace, there may be people who have physical or mental disabilities. At one of our recent business trips, after getting off the plane, we noticed a gentleman in a manually operated wheelchair pushing his wheelchair up a steep ramp in the terminal. We said, "Hello, would you like some help?" He said, "No, I think I got it, but I appreciate you asking." Our CEO was once conducting a live training program and a man sitting in the back of the room was blind. When it was time for lunch, everyone got up and walked out of the room. The blind man sat in the back with his seeing-eye dog. Shawn went back to the man said, "Hello, do you know where the lunchroom is located and how to get there?" The man chuckled and said, "No, I don't know where lunch is and neither does my dog!" What a wonderful sense of humor.

Even though this sounds like some sort of joke, it was a real situation that happened. It was puzzling that everyone else got up and left the room and didn't think about this man. Shawn then asked the man if he would like to take his arm so they could walk together to the lunchroom. He said, "I would appreciate that." The key point here is, if you see someone with disabilities who needs help, just politely ask if they need help. If the person says no, then don't. If yes, then help them cheerfully and with as much respect as you would want your loved ones to be treated. This is just simple human decency and kindness.

Tip 16: Just a note. Anytime anyone in the office does something kind for you like taking you out to lunch, celebrating your birthday or your work anniversary, or doing some sort of favor, you should send a handwritten thank-you note. Go to your favorite card store or your favorite stationery store or online and buy some thank-you cards that look professional and reflect your personality. When handwriting a thank-you note, make sure to mention: 1) your appreciation; 2) what they did for you specifically such as, Thank you so much for the wonderful scarf for my birthday"; and 3) how it made you feel. Find out the person's home address and send the thank-you note to their home; don't just put it in their inbox at their office. If you have to resort to a quick email to thank someone due to time constraints, that is acceptable but it would mean so much more to that person if you take time to actually handwrite a note. What a connection and impression you can make!

Tip 17: You have a gift. Many people ask me for advice about an appropriate gift to give someone in the workplace. If you're going to give someone a gift in the workplace, make sure it is an appropriate, modest gift. Gifts that appear too expense or inappropriate are embarrassing to receive at the workplace. Do your best to select something professional, pleasing, and something that would apply specifically to that person based on what you know about him or her. The idea is to show that you appreciate the person and that you have put thought into the gift.

Tip 18: Boss birthday or holiday. What do you do when it is your boss's birthday or a holiday? It certainly would be appropriate to give your boss a birthday card signed by everyone in the department, or to have everyone in your department take the boss out to lunch. You can take up a collection to give your boss a modest gift appropriate for him or her. Some bosses give gifts to their associates that are gender-neutral gifts and given to everyone on the team. This is also acceptable. If you are new to the company or organization, ask if there is a specific gift-giving policy.

> "Good manners are cost effective. They do not only increase the quality of life in the workplace, they contribute to employee morale, embellish the company image, and play a major role in generating profit."
> —LETITIA BALDRIGE

Final Thoughts

I have covered many aspects of effective communication, but truly there is much more—as human beings are constant communicators. I believe communication is the key to success in life both professionally and personally. If you really wish to connect with the world around you, then develop your communication skills using what you have learned in this field guide. I know amazing things will happen. You will:

- Get the job you want instead of losing it.
- Solve problems instead of creating them.
- Mend fences instead of destroying them.
- Heal relationships instead of ending them.
- End wars instead of fueling them.
- Create peace and joy instead of causing pain and sorrow.

It just takes you deciding to be a great communicator.

As Jim Rohn said, "Take advantage of every opportunity to practice your communication skills so that when important occasions arise, you will have the gift, the style, the sharpness, the clarity, and the emotions to affect other people."

About the Author

Rachael Doyle was born into a multigenerational family of successful entrepreneurs. In her early teens, she worked in the family business in several roles. In her late twenties, she co-founded and built a successful photography business in Michigan. Since then Rachael has worked in her own business or for other businesses for more than three decades and has learned many valuable lessons from her experiences. She has a passion for lifelong learning and enjoys sharing those lessons learned with readers through her books.

Rachael and her husband, Shawn, train professionals how to win at work. They would love to help you and your organization by providing the following:

- Training
- Speaking
- Executive coaching
- Consulting

Visit their website: www.shawndoyletraining.com. Feel free to contact Rachael at Rachael@ShawnDoyleTraining.com.

Tune in to their podcast: Winning Edge at Work with Shawn and Rachael Doyle. You can subscribe by signing up on all major podcast sites.